Like Those *who* Dream

Like Those *who* Dream

Sermons for Salford Mennonite Church
and Beyond

JAMES C. LONGACRE

Foreword by
Walter Brueggemann

Cascadia
Publishing House
Telford, Pennsylvania

copublished with
Herald Press
Scottdale, Pennsylvania

Cascadia Publishing House LLC orders, information, reprint permissions:
contact@cascadiapublishinghouse.com
1-215-723-9125
126 Klingerman Road, Telford PA 18969
www.CascadiaPublishingHouse.com

Like Those Who Dream
Copyright © 2009 by Cascadia Publishing House
a division of Cascadia Publishing House LLC, Telford, PA 18969
All rights reserved.
Copublished with Herald Press, Scottdale, PA
Library of Congress Catalog Number: 2008041484
ISBN 13: 978-1-931038-51-5; **ISBN 10:** 1-931038-51-1
Book design by Cascadia Publishing House
Cover design by Dawn Ranck

The paper used in this publication is recycled and meets the
minimum requirements of American National Standard for Information
Sciences—Permanence of Paper for Printed Library Materials, ANSI
Z39.48-1984.

Library of Congress Cataloguing-in-Publication Data
Longacre, James C., 1941-
Like those who dream : sermons for Salford Mennonite Church
and beyond / James C. Longacre ; foreword by Walter Brueggemann.
p. cm.
ISBN-13: 978-1-931038-51-5 (pbk. : alk. paper)
ISBN-10: 1-931038-51-1 (pbk. : alk. paper)
1. Mennonite Brethren Church--Sermons. 2. Sermons, American. I. Title.

BX8129.M376L66 2009
252'.097--dc22

2008041484

16 15 13 12 11 10 09   10 9 8 7 6 5 4 3 2 1

When the Lord
restored the fortunes of Zion,
we were like those who dream.
—Psalm 126:1

Contents

Foreword

As James C. Longacre observes in a sermon connecting the lives of Israelites in Babylon with those of North Americans today,

> The wisdom of the day may well have been that this is it. Get used to it. Make a buck where you can. Live for the next vacation. What's on TV? Are you having regular or decaf?
>
> So the prophet who would arouse these people out of their unimaginative conversation needed to speak with unusual power. Exceptional, imaginative, poetic language and musical cadence were needed. Thus, in the prophetic poetry again and again the words *awake, listen, hear, see* occur. "Sing, O barren one. . . . " "Ho, everyone who thirsts. . . . "

Showing us what it means to become *Like Those Who Dream*, Longacre himself practices arousing us out of our unimaginative conversations. Not often do oral sermons ring true in written form . . . but these do!

Not often do old sermons come clear with fresh contemporeneity . . . but these do!

Not often do preachers take up controversial issues and walk us into new freedom and new courage beyond our predilections . . . but this one does!

Not often is obedience cast in preaching as the good news of joy . . . but it happens here!

These sermons do all of that . . . and much more. It is no wonder that Longacre is a star preacher without calling attention to himself. These sermons will "do" very well for readers who care about good news and new life. They are gifts that keep on giving.

—*Walter Brueggeman*
  Columbia Theological Seminary
  September 24, 2008

Introduction

While there have been previous books of Mennonite sermons, the present one is unique in the history of both the Franconia and Lancaster Mennonite Conferences of southeastern Pennsylvania. From our European beginnings, we had prized simplicity in all things. In the 1840s a progressive preacher had been criticized for preaching a "studied sermon," and a century later one of our deacons sitting behind a western preacher using notes, had tugged at the visitor's coattail, muttering, "That is not done here." In fact, in the forty or fifty congregations of James Longacre's Franconia Conference, pre-written words from the pulpit were generally not welcome before the mid-twentieth century.

By 1992, however, when James came to the 275-year-old Salford Mennonite congregation near Harleysville, not only the surrounding farmscape but the expectations of the listeners themselves had changed. For half a century we had had young people going to college and beyond, and for the previous two decades we had had preaching by seminary-trained ministers. James himself had graduated from both Eastern Mennonite College (now University) and the graduate school of the Southern Baptist Baylor University. He had then honed his homiletic calling, beginning at his home congregation in the village of Bally at the northwest edge of the Franconia Conference area, and later at the larger congregation of Blooming Glen in Bucks County. His sense of the wider church was nurtured by his service as Conference Moderator and Coordinator.

Over his fifteen years at Salford, Jim shared the preaching task with a sequence of half a dozen assistants, including myself, who had shared the pulpit with Willis Miller for the previous twenty years. The present thoughts thus come from hearing Jim preach while seated behind him on the platform and later amid the congregation. From both perspectives I can bear testimony to the seriousness with which Jim approached this ministry.

Amid our increasingly generic suburban patterns, we heard sermonic echoes of a rural childhood, youth, and beginning ministry at Bally. With our pastor remaining a part-time farmer on a family homestead, we may have been the last local congregation to hear preaching that reflected the hands-on relation with the crops and heifers and farm auctions that flavored all our lives half a century ago. At the same time, Jim's service as chair of the board of our denominational Associated Mennonite Biblical Seminary at Elkhart, Indiana, and his evident reading of his *New York Times* set his words in the context of the broader picture of both church and world.

Those of us who listened for fifteen years will recall a favorite phrase, *the themes of the faith.* In fact Jim's sermons, seldom dwelling on process, procedure, or strategy, were always theme-oriented. He could not help exclaiming how "rich," "deep," and "broad" these themes are.

Next to that word came the repeated reminder that we were dealing with a "text." It was Jim's joy to let the ancient Word speak. He reads the letter carefully but listens beyond it to the canon-broad "music" of Scripture. What was humorously said of an old Franconia bishop—"He had one text—the whole Bible"—could be said in appreciation of Jim's range. A further compliment to the same rustic church servant applies equally to Jim's preaching: *Er is' bei'm Watt gebliwwe*—"He stuck by the Word."

Jim preaches a full gospel: the news of divine love that transforms both the personal and the social life of those who accept it. The substantial old issues are here in current expressions.

There's a special awareness too, of being a preacher at the threshold between an earlier Plain People's sobriety and today's freer and multicultural attitudes. As Jim put it, it could sometimes feel necessary in his preaching at Salford to "slip by" both the "accumulated prejudices" of past Mennonite tribal life and their opposite, the wider "society's bias against religious conviction." The tone may thus be non-judgmental, as the pastor in the preacher searches for "the softest language [he can] think of" without watering down the gospel. A familiar note is that of a gentle questioning: "Could it be?" or "Might it just be?" or "Have you ever noticed?" or "Have you ever imagined?" But true preaching is not about merely making hearers feel good about themselves. When exhorting Christians that are touchy about an authoritarian past, Jim reminds them frankly that the household of faith is to be "an uncommon people."

These sermons continually stress sensing the great Gospel themes in the small venues. The sermon titles are already reminders of this urge: "One of the smaller clans"; "In a place like Woxall"; "You never know." The other side of that small-great equation is a reiterated joy in the abundance, the superabundance—the plenitude—of God's grace in both Creation and Redemption. Of course it takes faith to accept the evidence. This is demonstrated in the way these sermons already celebrate, in lifting up the dream, the joy of fulfillment.

The thirty-two sermons in this book are taken from a corpus of more than five hundred digitally preserved manuscripts. The first and last ones are the actual first and last of the fifteen years at Salford. Reading them out of context of the series they came in of course affects the focus of the experience. And certainly, reading a sermon is not the same as hearing it while sitting among other listeners. The humorous inflections, the interjections, the interaction with the congregation, the recent congregational "moments" that have affected the atmosphere—are all missing. On the other hand, reading one sermon at a time can make it seem like just walking into a church to hear the Word for that day. Taken in at the reader's own meditative pace, sermons such as these can make inspiring devotional reading.

Because the preaching task was taken so seriously by this pastor, the Salford congregation has found it fitting, at James Longacre's retirement, to preserve a portion of its harvest. This is done both in appreciation for the preacher, and out of a desire to share with friends, Christian or otherwise, both locally and far beyond Salford Mennonite Church, the benefit of his heart-felt homiletic nurturing of our faith in Jesus Christ.

—*John L. Ruth*
  Vernfield, Pennsylvania

Author's Preface

Every Sunday the preacher is privileged to present again some part of a remarkable drama. Even the fully initiated cannot help but hold their breath. Will Sarah have a son after she laughed at the messenger? What good can Joseph do in Egypt in jail? Can engaging music be evoked in Babylon? Can anything good come out of Nazareth? A Messiah dead?

Central to the intriguing drama, whether on stage or off, slightly visible or fully mysterious, is God. What fascinates both the preacher and the listening community are the ways this God proceeds, time and again, in unexpected, unimaginable creating of new possibilities. Leading out of near certain dead-ends, *cul-de-sacs*, come new highways.

The story is so engaging that many gather regularly to hear it repeated. But each new encounter with the story is more than simple repetition. At different stages of life, amid changing social, political, economic contexts, the Scriptures spring forth anew in freshness and vibrancy.

Then, in steps small and large, careful listeners are drawn into the drama, not simply intrigued and inspired by the good story. The listeners now realize that the drama is unfinished and ongoing.

The listeners become more than a listening community. William Stacy Johnson wrote, "By becoming one with humanity in Jesus of Nazareth, God has determined not to be God without us."[1]

Thus the listening community moves from audience to stage.

For this to happen, deep concentration is required on Sundays. All week the people of faith live in a context where other powerful competing scripts, texts, ideologies dominate. Straight lines seem so obvious, so sensible: bigger is better, evil needs to be overcome by force, violence requires counter and greater violence. But the people of God, those with the biblical story lodged deeply in memory, see other options. Fully amazed at God's ways and believing that the creativity of God has not diminished, nor God's power come anywhere near exhaustion, the people of God wait, lean forward, hope, and work.

With this faith and hope embedded in their hearts, with the vision thus shaped, members of the Christian community choose to align their corporate life according to the texts. These themes become the major melodies of the music sung, and the lives lived.

Caught up in God's vision, the community of faith finds itself taking new turns, living out new options, dreaming new dreams. Since, in Christ, Jew and Gentile have been reconciled, it is of course possible for those who are very different to be brought together. If enemies are fed instead of hated, all kinds of possibilities arise. *"The just . . . live by faith."*

For fifteen years it was my privilege to consider the biblical drama and vision with the Salford Mennonite congregation of southeastern Pennsylvania. In Sunday morning sermons, wedding meditations, funeral services, membership classes, multiple teaching opportunities and conversations, I had the wonderful privilege to give witness to God's ways. Building on the faithful work of previous pastors and teachers in the congregation, I sought to steward the Word.

While the depth and breadth of Scripture always far exceeded my efforts to articulate its message fully, I was privileged to see the message take root. As Richard Lischer has described what happens, there was a "remarkable synergy of the spoken word and the life of the baptized community."[2]

The congregation lived the Word in special care for the mentally ill and a commitment to serve the developmentally disabled and the elderly. Teachers taught history and world cultures, not as viewed through American eyes, but from a global perspective. Business persons hired individuals who had previously failed. Young persons volunteered to serve—from Vietnam to Swaziland to Zambia. The Word continued to take on flesh.

To be sure, we did not see Satan fall entirely from heaven (Luke 10:18), but again and again the reigning ideologies of our time were questioned and countered, and new possibilities were offered.

In the sermons included in this volume, as in all my preaching, I tried to draw upon the whole of the Scriptures. Knowing that the Bible comes to us in very rich diversity, with delightful various melodies from multiple angles, I have sought to give voice to this richness.

Needless to say, the preacher draws from the fruit of countless imaginative and faithful interpreters of the faith of generations past and present. I am most grateful for this great multitude of diligent teachers and writers, from a number of whom I trust I have learned a little.

My thanks to John L. Ruth for his assistance in helping to select the sermons for this volume, for his editorial work, and for his ongoing encouragement and good counsel. I hereby also acknowledge with gratitude the fine work of Michael A. King of Cascadia Publishing House.

My wife, Ellen Rose Herr Longacre, has always had a keen ear for imaginative phrases, apt descriptions, the creative edge. She knows a good sermon when she hears it. I trust I have met her expectations occasionally.

—*James C. Longacre*
 Barto, Pennsylvania

Like
Those
who
Dream

Chapter 1

Hosanna from the Fifth Row

FIRST SERMON AFTER INSTALLATION AT SALFORD
Palm Sunday, April 12, 1992
Matthew 21:1-17

In this Palm Sunday parade, where do you imagine you would have been? Perhaps you see yourself as part of the crowd that "went ahead," as noted in verse 9. Or would you be among the supporters in the rear?

I think I would have made it to the parade route and probably stood along the roadside. And if the crowds along the curb or the banks had been ten deep, you would have found me in about the fifth row.

I'm not one to get overly enthusiastic. I like to keep my feet on the ground. I'm a little suspicious of any kind of crowd mentality, be it flag- or palm-branch-waving. Yet I hate to miss real action. So the fifth row is about right.

The fifth row is a kind of Mennonite position. We choose not to be too conspicuous. Surely we do not wish to cause trouble. If there is big trouble, we'll be there to clean up. We make our contribution but hate to be the focus of attention. The fifth row is about right.

If I had my choice and could have positioned myself ideally, I would have also wanted to get behind a family—preferably a family whose parents were of better than average stature and the children quite small. Then, depending on how things turned out,

I could have positioned myself accordingly. I could be behind the children and be fairly visible, or, if things got a little embarrassing, I could have ducked behind the parents incognito-like.

This Palm Sunday scene has a kind of ambiguity about it. Even today in the Christian church we do not know whether we should celebrate it with full trumpets blaring—or sort of skip over it and call it Passion Sunday.

You see, we cannot quite tell what this crowd was up to. What were these shouts about? Was this genuine worship? Were they honestly and truly and finally recognizing Jesus for who and what he was? Or was this a political rally with religious overtones?

Some even doubt the sincerity of the crowd. Fickle, some would say—shouting "Hosanna!" one day and a few days later, "Crucify!" I'm not ready to cast that judgment. There may well have been two quite different crowds.

But in any case the shouts are a little unclear. What did they want? It is not fully evident what "Hosanna" meant, or what it may have meant to those in the first or the fifth row.

One translation of the word *hosanna* is "Save Now." But "save now" from what? Then there is this "Son of David" theme, which may well strike a more political than a religious note, although God and Country were closely intertwined.

What Did They Want?

Now we know why the multitudes were in and around Jerusalem. It was annual pilgrimage time, Passover time. The faithful, the pious, and probably the not quite so pious came to Jerusalem to remember the signal event in Jewish history—the marvelous deliverance from Egypt. Jesus came, too.

But we wonder why this crowd gathered to welcome Jesus. Was it totally spontaneous? Might some group have planned it?

It appears that those at the parade route had some acquaintance with Jesus. What did they expect of him now?

We can well imagine that some in the crowd had heard Jesus preach and teach. Perhaps they had been genuinely moved by the freshness, the creative edge of his message. The notes of repentance, forgiveness, hope, faith, and more struck a chord deep within their beings.

Undoubtedly, some of those who had been healed, together with their relatives and friends, were there along the parade route. Had you or I been blind and healed by Jesus, surely we would have been eternally grateful and joined in this rally for Jesus. So blind Bartimeaus with his clan, his *freundschaft*, may well have been there.

And those who were fed along the sea—the 5,000 and the 4,000—how could they have forgotten that experience? I can also imagine that the local business booster club from Nazareth may have shown up. So though Jesus was not the hero in the local synagogue, surely some would have been proud of the local son.

Oh, there could have been an assortment of others. Who more likely than Zacchaeus to have been there, cutting off the palm branches?

Still, the more important question is, What did they expect of Jesus? So they shouted "Save now," but from what? Again, of course, we can only speculate.

There may well have been those who still wished for more bread. You recall in reading Mark's Gospel in particular that Jesus chided those who sought only bread; he hoped to offer more. But let us not condemn. There were those in Palestine who were genuinely hungry.

Perhaps some wanted political freedom. The Romans weren't the worst political overlords in history, but even benevolent rulers get under the skin. The decade following Jesus' life would hear loud "down with the Romans" cries, and perhaps these seeds were already here in the palm-waving cheers.

Others in the crowd may have been weary of the religious hierarchy. You note in this text that in the cleansing of the temple Jesus hardly rated the religious system with an A+. Surely there was unrest and resentment over how the well-connected religious leaders seemed to profit from the system. So there was undoubtedly the sentiment that Jesus could restore true faith and piety, and many wished for that. Had not John the Baptist called for genuine repentance and social change from top to bottom?

There were those who wished for better times. For the rural families times were tough. The economy had been stuck at zero growth not for two years but decades. Surely deep in their souls they had heard the cries of Amos and wished that the prophet of Nazareth would bring economic justice.

Let us not be judgmental. Intertwined with all of these political and economic dreams there were undoubtedly genuine religious stirrings. Religion had gotten a little tight. The scribes were a bit dull—their religion was rehearsal. The Pharisees, seen even in the best light, tended to be maintainers of the status quo.

Amid this scene, Jesus had struck a chord. No prophet, all admitted, had risen in Israel for a long time. There was genuine thirst for the new visitation of God.

Then, as in any age, there were those burdened with guilt. Having sought to live by the law, having hoped to live righteous lives, they had been brought in the ebb and flow of life to failures and disappointments. These folks surely had heard Jesus' words, "Come to me all you that labor and are heavy laden and I will give you rest." These too longed for spiritual rest.

So we can understand why the people had gathered. There were reasons enough to wish for change. The reasons for the cry "Hosanna" may have greatly varied, but reasons there were. And hopes were stirred as the man Jesus of Nazareth rode on a colt that day.

What Do *We* Want?

Whether we sit on the first or the twenty-fifth row or stand up front, what is it we expect of Jesus this Palm Sunday? What is the meaning of our Hosanna? From what do we want to be saved? Might it be that we are not totally unlike the people along the road outside Jerusalem? Our hopes and dreams may be as varied as theirs, but hopes and dreams we have, nevertheless.

Perhaps we wish for economic stability. A little more bread would help many in this society. Job security, or just plain a job, is the wish of more than a few.

Or maybe we wish for a change in the settings of our lives. We are restless with the vocations we find ourselves in, or at least the positions we find ourselves in. Or is it that the work environment lacks challenge?

For others, family relationships might be the focus of what we would have Jesus change. If only a parent, a spouse, a son, a daughter would be what we would wish them to be!

Amid this and more, is there perhaps as well a religious stirring, a holy restlessness, a disquiet at the center of our lives? We, too, line the road to Jerusalem and in many and varied ways, demonstratively or less so, cry to Jesus for change.

Jesus accepts the hosannas. The Palm Sunday parade is not condemned. To be sure, the motives were mixed. Some were there out of deep love and appreciation of Jesus, and some were there to raise a ruckus, hoping to encourage Jesus to take on the establishment in Jerusalem. Whatever the motives, on Palm Sunday Jesus accepts the stirrings of the heart.

When the religious leaders (v. 15) "heard the children crying out in the temple, 'Hosanna to the Son of David,' they became angry, and said to him, 'Do you not hear what these are saying?'"

Jesus said to them, "Yes, have you never read, 'out of the mouths of infants and nursing babies you have prepared praise for yourself'?"

Or, in Luke's account, Jesus responded to the complaint this way: "I tell you, if these were silent, the stones would shout out" (Luke 19:40). Jesus graciously accepted the hearts' stirrings on Palm Sunday.

So, too, he accepts our hearts' yearnings. On another occasion Jesus quoted the prophet Isaiah: "He will not break a bruised reed or quench a smoldering wick." Whatever stage our spiritual quest, Jesus would fan it into flame. Thus he reaches out to us, half-hearted, and hunkered down in the fifth row.

But we are not left there. Palm Sunday is not the end. Not by any means.

Not all is well on Palm Sunday, even with the hosannas all over the place and palm branches waving, and lovely children's music. Jerusalem is hardly at peace. The temple is anything but a house of prayer. Instead of praying, the religious leaders are plotting. And having just experienced the lovely parade, Jesus just about blows up in the temple.

So Palm Sunday is nice—but not enough. Jesus did not condemn the hopes and dreams—but he did not answer them all. Not all the hungry were fed. Economic prosperity did not come to all. The Romans remained fully in power. The reign of David remained a romantic dream. The temple, cleansed momentarily, nevertheless was horribly destroyed just a few decades later.

The children were left to sing another day. We assume the palm branches grew back. (Although in another text the fig tree died.)

We have been around long enough to know, too, that many of our own hopes, wishes, desires, and cries remain unanswered. The text for today ends with these words: "He left them, went out of the city to Bethany, and spent the night there."

So is that the way it is? He hears our hopes and dreams, he acknowledges our cries, then leaves? Is that all there is—a brief pat on the back, then abandonment?

In the book of James the writer suggests that "we do not have because we do not ask," or, much more seriously, we do not have because "we ask amiss. "

Is it not true that much of our asking is that things out there be changed? We want our environment changed, we want other people to change, we want to be there and not here. We perhaps ask amiss.

It is on Thursday evening that Jesus returns. The Last Supper, the Feet Washing, the Garden, the Trial, all the disciples leave—then the cross.

It might well be that we ask amiss. More specifically, it might be that we do not ask enough. We want change out there. But Jesus would change what we failed to ask for—that we be changed.

The Good Friday service will focus on the one who left on Palm Sunday, but returned on Good Friday. This is the one who leaves many of our hopes and dreams unanswered but offers freely what we need most.

Martin Luther King Jr. said, "Whom you would change you must first love."[3] The writer of John's gospel described Jesus at the Last Supper this way: "Having loved his own who were in the world, he loved them to the end."

What he offers is what we hadn't thought to ask. And the way he offers it is truly astounding. One hymn writer asks, "What wondrous love is this, O my soul?" Another exclaims, "Hallelujah, what a Savior!"

Chapter 2

To Prophesy or
to Keep Silent: Women
in Ministry

SERIES: WOMEN IN MINISTRY

September 20, 1992

Genesis 1:26-31; Joel 2:28-29; Galatians 3:23-29; 1 Timothy 2:8-15

Years ago in some Mennonite congregations the sermons at times went fairly long. Around the Sunday dinner table in our family we would grumble about these long sermons and ask, Did the preacher really need to preach from Genesis to Revelation in one sermon? Take heart; today I will only go from Genesis to 1 Timothy.

The issue at hand, as has been duly announced, is the question of women in leadership, or more precisely here at Salford, women as part of the pastoral team. Over the next months, years, there will likely be additions to the pastoral team. Can women be considered for any of these responsibilities?

We'll want to come to some resolution of this matter as a congregation. We'll want to speak carefully and listen intensely to the many and varied understandings, viewpoints, and experiences. You are all needed in this discussion. Your perspectives and questions deserve to be heard and considered. We will strive to work at this matter together.

On any question and issue in the life of the church we rightly begin with consideration of the biblical perspective. We rightly ponder the story of God and God's people. We pay particular attention to the life and teachings of Jesus. We ponder the writings of the apostles.

Thus today, on this matter we turn to the Scriptures. Understandably we cannot pursue every applicable text, nor consider even a few texts at great depth. We will rather try to sense the broad themes of Scripture, the direction, the movement of Scripture as it might apply to this issue.

Now some rightly ask, "Why does this issue emerge at all?" For many, the Scriptures seem quite clear. Understandings have been in place for centuries—why make an issue of things that have historically been quite settled?

Let it be acknowledged at the outset that there are straightforward, clear biblical texts that suggest women have important roles and are to be fully respected, but that in God's design leadership in the church is not one of these roles.

The text read from 1 Timothy 2 is rather direct: "I permit no woman to teach or to have authority over a man; she is to keep silent." This is not the only such text. One finds comparable statements in other New Testament writings, the Pastoral Epistles in particular.

This text and similar ones seem to represent the actual practice of the early church. Jesus chose twelve men as disciples. The key leaders of the early emerging church, at least the ones we can name, were men.

Further, it is observed, these perspectives on roles and positions of authority have to do with concerns of order in the family and society. The critical issue, it is argued, is not that of value and worth, but rather of role and function. Obviously, for social units to function, whether a society, a family, or a congregation, there needs to be some sense of leadership and responsibility. Thus it is suggested that it is God's design that there be order, and the order established by God in the family and the church is man—and then woman.

Fair-minded people would readily acknowledge that this order has been wrongly used. Many who have taken up this responsibility of leadership and authority have become authoritarian, insensitive, inconsiderate.

Those who agree with this sense of order and authority in the family and church note that other New Testament texts provide powerful checks against inappropriate and inconsiderate seizing of authority. Specifically, Paul's call to mutual submission in Ephesians 5, and his call that husbands love their wives as Christ loved the church, are surely provisions to counter tendencies toward insensitivity, harshness, and heavy-handedness.

All of which is to say that persons who understand the Scriptures to teach that it is part of God's ordering that there be some differentiation of roles and responsibilities, that this includes perspectives on leadership and authority and means that men are to be involved in the pastoral roles in the church rather than women, have scriptural perspectives for these understandings. In truth, the most explicit biblical texts dealing with the issue of women in ministry are on the side of prohibiting women in ministry.

But just about the time that things seem settled here—just at the time that one has lined up the biblical texts and become comfortable with these perspectives of appropriate sequences of order—another biblical melody sounds ever so gently. In an unruly world the buck needs to stop somewhere. Apparently God set up things to work. And to make them work, God put men in one role and women in another (both roles important, but different). But just as all this seems settled common sense, one remembers that some of the more compelling statements of Scripture itself came from women.

I think of the song of Miriam in the Old Testament, or the marvelous song of Mary recorded in Luke 1 which the church refers to as the Magnificat. If women are to keep silent, why are these words of women included in Holy Writ? If women are not to teach, why have we been taught by the songs and speeches of women from Holy Scripture?

If in God's order women are not to lead men, why do we have the example of Deborah as a judge in the Old Testament? What shall we do with the examples of women prophesying in both Old and New Testament?

And how shall we interpret Paul's references in his writings to women as co-workers, and Paul's clear indication that Aquilla and Priscilla shared in the leadership of a congregation, with Priscilla mentioned first in several of these references?

It should be stated additionally that in reading the Gospels one has to be struck by the frequency wherein the gospel writers record incidents of Jesus interacting with women. One might note in particular the story of Mary and Martha, in which Jesus commends Mary for her taking interest in his teachings.

All of this is in a religious context in which women were assigned a secondary position. In the temple in Jerusalem, when people came to worship there were different areas for different people. There was the court of the Gentiles. Then there was the court where women could come, then the place for Jewish men, then the place for the priests, then the place where the high priest could be but once a year.

But Jesus invites women into his very presence. They need not ask of their husbands at home but are invited to make inquiry directly of him. And Jesus commends them.

So what are we to do with these streams within the biblical text? What are we to do with clear texts prohibiting women to teach, on the one hand, and on the other, examples of women speaking, teaching, prophesying, leading—fully recorded as part of the whole biblical record?

If you were the preacher this morning, how would you solve the apparent dilemma? Women are to keep silent, yet Mary's song rings down the centuries from Scripture itself. Women are not to lead, yet Deborah did, and quite effectively. Women are to be saved by childbearing, yet Mary sits at the feet of Jesus listening and learning and Jesus commends her. Women are not to be leaders, but Paul writes in Romans 16, "Greet Prisca and Aquila, who work with me in Christ Jesus."

What is going on here, and how shall we interpret?

Permit me to humbly offer several perspectives. None is conclusive in and of itself, and perhaps even all of these together will not fully resolve the dilemma nor be fully persuasive.

To begin, note that the first explicit text suggesting that men are to have authority over women occurs in Genesis 3, which is God's statement to Adam and Eve because of their disobedience, their failure to live harmoniously with God and with creation. Genesis 3:16 reads that God said to the woman, "I will greatly increase your pangs in childbearing; in pain you shall bring forth children, yet your desire shall be for your husband, and he shall rule over you."

This suggests that the perspectives of hierarchy, rule, authority, over-and-under, subjection, have more to do with the

Fall, with disobedience, with sin, than with the bold and marvelous vision of God. To be sure, the teachings of hierarchy and rule are God-given, they are surely in the Bible, but they are accommodations because of sin; they are necessary in a fallen world; they are concessions to a fallen humanity.

Let me illustrate with another biblical example. Romans 13 is a text which fully sanctions governmental authority and even the use of the sword in the interest of maintaining order and control in society.

Is law and order, maintained by threats of jail, maintained by threats of violence, God's highest will and desire? No, these are concessions, part of God's ordering because of an unruly and fallen humanity.

One sees today in Somalia, or in the former Yugoslavia, the consequences of the breakdown of governing authority. Chaos rules.

So I am suggesting that order in society and the family, which are part of the biblical record, and have their point of origin in God, is God's design as a result of sin. Such ordering is necessary in a fallen world.

But God has a more excellent way for God's people. There is a higher vision. The vision of mutual esteem, mutual respect, mutual submission, love, equal value, pushes itself through the biblical record again and again as this higher vision.

One thinks of several other divisions, other hierarchical arrangements, which are gradually broken down by the gospel. In the New Testament one recalls the struggles with Jew and Gentile. In the early church these were real struggles. Other familiar examples include preferential treatment for Jews while the Gentiles had second class citizenship—until the church came to realize that in Christ there is neither Jew nor Greek

Or it took centuries for slavery to be broken down. The Galatians vision was not fulfilled even in the context of the New Testament, where at points the slave system itself remained uncontested, even though inherent within the New Testament itself is the clear undercutting of this institution. Surely the early church heard the text, "In Christ there is neither slave nor free," but it took a while until that institution of owner and slave gave way.

So the first observation is that the arrangement of hierarchy, the notion that men should rule over women, is a consequence of the Fall. It is an arrangement which was God-given—but because of sin, because of fallenness.

In God's new community the consequences of the Fall are to be rolled back. Thus, in Christ there is no longer "male and female, for all of you are one in Christ."

A second biblical perspective to note is this: In the experience of the people of God, women were afforded far higher status and recognition than in the non-Hebraic social context in which they lived. To repeat, it is clear that in the Old Testament times Jewish women had a far higher position than their counterparts in the cultures surrounding the people of Israel. One sees in the laws of the Old Testament specific guidelines protecting women from arbitrary and thoughtless actions of husbands and society. Whereas women in the various other cultures of biblical times would have been seen as little more than property, among God's people women were afforded some measure of dignity and respect.

In the New Testament, when one keeps both Roman and Greek culture in mind, one has to be impressed by the way Jesus openly engaged women in his ministry and by its being fully recorded by the gospel writers. One suspects that even the Jewish leaders were offended by the way women again and again were included in the circle with the disciples.

One should note how, in the discussion concerning divorce, Jesus' concern rested with the rights of women.

In the early church women were afforded roles of deaconess, co-workers, and much more. This was done in the context of Jewish restrictions.

One can thus conclude that where God's movement is pressing in, the status of women is higher than in the surrounding culture. If that is the movement of the whole of Scripture, we may well conclude that the church has the privilege and responsibility to continue in that development.

Today's compelling text from the prophet Joel seems to gather up this underground stream in the biblical tradition—this abiding vision that each and all of God's people, irrespective of gender, are freed and empowered to participate actively and enthusiastically in the mission of the church. Whereas amid the world where all kinds of unequal status and positions exist, in the age of God's Spirit these divisions give way.

What a vision: where young and old, men and women, black and white, those with black hair and those with red, those from two-parent homes and those with one parent, are all free and empowered to participate in the call of Jesus!

All are needed. Every hand should be put to work. The kingdom needs us all.

Chapter 3

You Never Know: Waiting in Advent

ADVENT
November 28, 1993
Isaiah 64:1-9; Mark 13:32-37

Our family doctors in my growing up years were a husband and wife combination: George and Faith Baver from Pennsburg. When you were ill, you went to their home and office during office hours. There were no appointments as such. So when you got there you sat in the waiting room. During cold or flu seasons the waiting room was generally full.

Waiting.

There was always conversation in the waiting room. First off, since there was no receptionist, you had to figure out for yourself your particular order to see a doctor. There was no number to take and then wait for it to be called. No, you had to figure out who was the person that came in the waiting room before you. Of course, you had not been there to see who came before you. You had to ask.

The situation was further complicated. There were two doctors but only one waiting room. Did you want to see Dr. George or Dr. Faith? (In the waiting room of course it was simply George or Faith.) You might find there were seven ahead of you to see George and five ahead of you to see Faith. You may have had a preference for George, but how long did you want to wait?

Having engaged in conversation concerning your particular order, it was easy to converse about other things. What was wrong with you, for example? So before long not only did you know your order, you knew the ailments of almost everybody else in the room, and of course the ailments of a whole variety of people in the community, who, if the description of the ailments was accurate, surely should have been in the waiting room with you, waiting to see George or Faith.

Now it was also known that Dr. George was a blunt and forthright doctor. Most of the time you could hear little through the door between the waiting room and Dr. George's office, but if George had a particular point to make, it could be rather easily heard. No one in the waiting room wanted to let on to listening, but the conversation would subside when some patient in Dr. George's office got lectured. Of course, you knew who the patient was, since it was the fifth or seventh patient before you.

The wait in the waiting room was often long. If you were really sick, you began to wonder whether many in the waiting room, particularly those ahead of you, were really sick or simply enjoying the drama of the waiting room.

Today is the first Sunday of Advent, which marks the beginning of the church year. Now isn't it strange that the cycle of celebrations, the remembrances of the significant events of the Christian faith, should begin when nothing is happening? Why not begin the church year with the big events of the faith—such as Easter or Pentecost? Why begin the church year when nothing is happening, or at least almost nothing is happening?

But the church year begins at Advent; it begins with a period of waiting—four Sundays, four weeks.

What might happen when we wait? We'll consider that in drawing on the text from Isaiah 64.

The setting of this text, some scholars suggest, may be Babylon. The children of Israel lament their plight. The glory days are gone. The beautiful city of Jerusalem lies largely in ruin. Worse, the temple is destroyed. The lights have pretty well gone out.

Worse still is the crisis of faith. Had not God promised much to Israel? Was not the temple central to the promise? Why did the God of Exodus now look weak against the gods of Babylon?

So in Israel's waiting in Babylon, in their frustrations with their lot, their prophet cries out again to their God,

> O that you would tear open the heavens and come down,
>> so that the mountains would quake at your presence. . . .
> to make your name known to your adversaries,
>> so that the nations might tremble at your presence!

Here is this plea to God to act as of old—to do again the wonders of the past.

In their frustration and anxiety, the people even tend to blame God—"you were angry, and we sinned; because you hid yourself we transgressed." (v. 5). Or again in verse 7 we learn that "you have hidden your face from us, and have delivered us into the hand of our iniquity."

It is in waiting that we become quite aware of our situation. While waiting we have occasion to consider the conditions of life. In this period of Advent we surely must acknowledge that not all is well in our world. We in fact do well to let our minds circle the globe and note the pain and anguish of our time. The litany of suffering and sorrow is broad and deep. We have heard particularly of the pain and suffering in Haiti last Sunday and in parts of Africa on Wednesday evening. The news reminds us of the tragedy and suffering in the former Yugoslavia. We read of the painful adjustments in the former Soviet Union.

In our land, at this time of year, there is a burst of concern for the poor and homeless—and thank God for even temporary compassion—but the systemic problems remain unaddressed as more and more slip below the poverty line. Meanwhile Wichita, Kansas, last week passed its 1992 record number of shootings, with six weeks to go yet this year.

In our period of waiting we become aware of our own situations, our own physical, emotional, and spiritual situation. In our waiting we realize anew our lives are filled, yet in some ways empty. We are both satisfied yet longing, happy but anxious, individuals of faith yet worried.

In our times of anxiety and frustration we, like the exiles in Babylon, cry to God to do something. We may well long for ages past. We may wish again for the old-time religion. We may long for earlier eras. We may cry for the return of former days. We might even blame God.

So at Advent we wait. While waiting we are to watch. Our New Testament text from Mark 13:32-37 calls for even more intensity in our waiting. Admittedly, this is a text dealing with the second Advent, the second coming of Christ, but it is also appropriately an Advent text: the attitude called for is an Advent attitude.

Throughout Scriptures there comes warning after warning that there are those who have eyes to see but do not see, ears to hear but do not hear. So there is the call for watchfulness.

Might it be that those who were calling anew for God to tear open the heavens, those who were hoping that God would shake the earth again, were looking at the wrong place? There is nothing wrong with the old-time religion except that God might choose to work in new ways. Those impressed only by God's big miracles may miss the thousand little ones.

Therein lies the reason to watch. *You never know* when or where or how God might work anew.

You see, the season of waiting is not one of simply putting in time. This is not simply "so many days until Christmas" which we cross off on the calendar to get by until *the* day comes.

The season of Advent is one for waiting in the sense of anticipation. Indeed it is a time for actively watching, because *you never know* when, or where, or how. A commentator writes:

> The word "watch" reaches into the whole spread of life. Someone has said that the worst "ism" in the world is not racism or communism but somnambulism. There are so many forms of sleepwalking—the glazed eyes which never notice that one's ideals are being whittled away, one's purposes being pared down; never notice the evil forces in the world gaining strength. *Watch and pray* against the sin that so easily trips us up, the compromise with wrong, so reasonable in the beginning, so deadly in the end. *Watch*, lest we neglect the renewal of life in communion with God, lest our sympathies harden. *Watch*, lest the great opportunities for service to God's kingdom come and pass by, unseen and unseized.[4]

Advent teaches us that precisely when it appears that nothing is happening, incredibly much is happening. Zechariah cannot speak. Elizabeth becomes pregnant. Mary sings. Taxes are being collected. The towns are crowded. Visitors are turned away. How silently, how silently the wondrous gift is given. Ignatius spoke of what "was wrought in the silence of God." Or the hymn writer referred to that which was "long beforehand."

So it may be with our lives. What appears to be nothing, what strikes us as difficult, this pain and that, this frustration and that, this obstacle and that—*you never know*. It may be "in the evening, or at midnight, or at the cockcrow, or at dawn. . . ." that God chooses a new visitation. *You never know.*

Which experience is an occasion for new steps of faith? Which event in our lives will be an occasion for a new realization of God's grace and love? Which life experience is going to be the new ingredient that reconfigures our lives? One wonders how many times the Lord may have been present and we did not know. We had not watched,

There are no off-duty hours, no circumstance off-limits to God's potential visitation. It may be in times of joy. It may be in times of pain. At midnight or at dawn. *You never know.*

Advent is an occasion to wait. We wait not in despair. We wait in hope. It has happened before. As we wait, and watch, and hope, lo and behold in unexpected ways, in "who would have thought it" kinds of events, the Lord comes anew. You never know.

Chapter 4

Will God Judge Rightly?

August 7, 1994
Luke 16:19-31; Romans 2:1-11

I remember the scene distinctly. It was one of those terribly hot and humid days of July a number of years ago, not unlike the kind of weather we have endured for the past few weeks. Our oldest son and I were stacking hay almost up against the roof in the barn. It gets hot there. It was very hot. My son had completed his sophomore or junior year of college—which is about the time when the values, teachings, and beliefs put forward by the family and the church are rolled over a bit, examined, questioned, pondered.

And so out of the blue, there in the stuffy, oppressively hot hay mow my son asked, "Dad, do you believe in hell?" Now the hot hay mow is hardly my favorite place for a theological conversation, and hell is not my favorite topic.

Actually, I would rather not even talk about hell in church. I much prefer to preach on the great themes of God's love, patience, kindness, mercy, and grace. These are the themes that stir the heart and imagination. These are the rich themes of the Scriptures, the surprising story of God.

In truth these are the themes that should be sounded most frequently and compellingly, for again and again in powerful story and imagery the Scriptures picture God as the father looking, looking down the road for the return of the son, as the employer who pays a full wage for those who labor only briefly in the vineyard. In the great crucifixion scene Jesus announces to the penitent thief on the cross, "Today you shall be with me in paradise." This is the story we preach, and preach it we must and do so with joy.

God's defining characteristic is love—steadfast , abiding, abounding love—reaching out earnestly, compassionately, enduringly. There is a wideness in God's mercy. Undoubtedly we shall all be wonderfully surprised as to whom God is able to gather into the kingdom, and I hope everlastingly grateful that we slipped in.

But amid this very dominant theme of Scripture there is— what shall we call it?—a sub-theme. Amid the marvelous melodies of love and grace, there is from time to time dissonance. In the great soaring themes of salvation there are also shadows, warnings, cautions. The language is graphic—fire, brimstone, weeping, desolation, and more.

Actually, the biblical texts referring to judgment are many. The last chapter of the last book of the Old Testament begins with these words: "See, the day is coming, burning like an oven, when all the arrogant and all evildoers will be stubble; the day that comes shall burn them up, says the Lord of hosts, so that it will leave them neither root nor branch" (Mal. 4:1).

The theme of judgment runs through the New Testament as well. Jesus spoke of it directly and in parables. The preaching of Acts includes warnings of judgment. Paul refers to judgment in most of his letters. The Pastoral Epistles add to the discussion. And of course the Book of Revelation uses vivid and dramatic language.

So what is a preacher to do? Shall we stay on the positive side and leave these texts for private reflection? Shall we, as some do, ascribe these references of judgment to the imaginations of first-century people? Shall we offer some kind of universalism which might suggest that in some marvelous way God will ultimately find some way to bring all peoples safely home?

Historically, the mainstream of the Christian tradition has held to the understanding of double destination—eternal life and eternal punishment. Is that now outdated? Did we misunderstand? Are there other interpretations?

Taking all of this out of the realm of theology and placing the issue squarely before us, the issue is quite pointedly this: Does it matter what we believe and how we live? Are there consequences here in this life and/or in the age to come for good or bad behavior?

Permit me to reflect on judgment in three ways. First, I'll note that there is already a measure of judgment in this age. Second, I'll draw attention to the texts read, particularly Romans 2, to reflect on the judgment yet to come. Finally I'll risk a few comments on the nature of the punishment.

In all of these matters I'll need to speak with a measure of caution and reserve, admitting that we do not understand fully the ways of God.

We can say with some confidence that even within the observable, within our own life experiences, there is a measure of judgment. It does matter how we live. Wrong choices do have consequences here and now. Let a few examples illustrate. The tobacco and liquor industries try to deny it, but excessive use of alcohol and tobacco do have direct consequences.

It is possible to pursue wrong habits and pay a price. How we eat and what we eat are important. How much stress we choose to live with does affect our well-being.

Dishonesty, shady dealings, and taking advantage of others have a way of turning back on us. Cheating on one's spouse hardly develops more harmonious and deepened marital relationships. The Scriptures suggest, "Be sure your sins will find you out."

On the wider scene, there is a measure of judgment within history. The Old Testament writers, in reflecting on the rise or fall of empires, saw within them the sovereignty of God. The imagery used at times was that the cup of God's wrath would fill up and enough was enough. Others suggested that evil had a way of causing its own undoing.

The Old Testament writers saw the rise and fall of Israel—the experience of defeat, destruction, and captivity—as evidence of the judgment of God.

So judgment is not entirely a. future phenomenon. It is within the ebb and flow of life itself. The moral values we espouse, how we treat others, what visions and goals we pursue—these do matter.

Now a certain caution needs to be offered. While we do affirm that there is judgment within history, while we assert that some things have negative consequences, the Scriptures consistently caution against our presuming to have adequate wisdom, or moral clarity, or freedom from self-deception, to qualify us to act as judge. We have an amazing tendency to think we see clearly the faults of others while remaining wholly blind to our own failures, sins, and shortcomings. Henry Wadsworth Longfellow wrote: "We judge ourselves by what we feel capable of doing; others judge us by what we have done."[5] Indeed we often tend to condemn in others that which is a particular tendency to failure within ourselves.

In the text from Romans 2, Paul, speaking to the Jews, suggests that they in judging the Gentiles condemn themselves, for they are doing the very same things. As Paul (in Rom. 1) had given a listing of the sins of the Gentiles, noting their dramatic wickedness, one can imagine the Jews saying, "Right on!"

But Paul abruptly turns the tables. Whereas he had said that the Gentiles had failed to live up to the moral standards and expectations of which they were aware, he adds that the Jews had likewise failed to live up to the light that they had. Thus they were in no position to judge.

WHAT OF THE JUDGMENT TO COME?

Judgment within history is imperfect, or at least appears so. It at least seems that some who live particularly evil and harmful lives get off rather easily. And some whose lives appear to be good and gracious suffer one hardship after another. Is then the picture of a final judgment simply a projection of some human need to see fairness?

No, the Scriptures frequently cite the expectation that the time will come when there will be a fair and final judgment. Let a few aspects of this expectation be noted.

All will be judged. The clear biblical expectation is that each and all, rich and poor, those heretofore dead and those living at the end of the age, will be judged. No one has a free ticket. No one has a pass. No one slides by Peter, or whoever the gate-keeper is. There are no special doors for VIP's. Mennonites have no special status. All will stand in the presence of the Lord of all.

The issue for consideration is essentially what we have done. That is the clear story in the account of Jesus of the judgment as recorded in Matthew 25. The basis of the judgment is how we have treated others. It is not our academic degrees, not our religious piety, but our deeds of love, kindness, and mercy.

Even in Paul's letter here to the Romans, when Paul argues vigorously in later chapters that we are not saved by our works, rather only by our faith, he nevertheless says that we will be judged by our deeds. Verse 6 states: "For he will repay according to each one's deeds."

In the penetrating light of God's truth all humankind will stand exposed. It will be as though an MRI machine will reveal who and what we are and how we have lived. Later in this chapter Paul adds that even the "secret thoughts" will be examined (v. 16).

There will be fairness. Paul says in verse 11, "For God shows no partiality." There will be no sweet talk, no getting in by virtue of one's good looks or persuasive personality. "For he will repay according to each one's deeds: to those who by patiently doing good seek for glory and honor and immortality, he will give eternal life; while for those who are self-seeking and who obey not the truth but wickedness, there will be wrath and fury" (vv. 6-8).

WILL THERE BE FIRE?

How serious is it if one doesn't quite qualify for entrance into heaven? How bad is the other place?

Some suggest that it is bad, but not for long. Using the text from Malachi, these would argue that the evil ones are simply destroyed—in the language of Malachi, burned root and branch.

Others would suggest that God will find some way to redeem even those who in this life rejected Jesus. They would cite texts that suggest Jesus between his death and resurrection descended even into hell. Others look to the promise that in the age to come ultimately every knee shall bow and all will recognize Christ as Lord.

One must exercise caution here, for the biblical references are filled with colorful imagery which should hardly be interpreted with absolute literalness. When the glories of heaven are described, the writer uses the most extravagant of language—golden streets, pearly gates. We would anticipate cool breezes, wonderful music. Doubtless the refugees of Rwanda would think of food and drink.

Likewise, when the place of separation from God is described, the absolute worst imagery is employed: the ever-burning fires at the garbage pit outside Jerusalem, utter darkness, and more.

One of the most intriguing aspects of the text from Luke 13 is the knowledge of opportunity missed. Can you imagine anything more haunting, frustrating, than to realize that the train has been missed and there is no other? Helmut Thieliecke writes: "Hell is simply the situation in which we must recognize God as God without being able to come to him." Or again, "To have to look at the spring of life without being able to drink from it. That hurts! That is to suffer the torment of an exile from which there is no return."[6] Another writer states: "Hell is truth seen too late—duty neglected in its season."[7]

I have no need to paint the picture of the state of the unrepentant in graphic terms. Is it not troublesome enough to think of a situation where the magnetic field of God's love and grace is withdrawn? Paul in Romans 1 pictures God's wrath as simply letting people on their own, where the gravitational pull of their sin takes them where it will, where hate multiplies hate, degrading passions multiply degrading passions, where utter selfishness has full reign.

Is that fair? Can a merciful God punish the wicked?

Is God to be blamed, is God unjust, is God unfair if, having extended the word of welcome throughout life and having been ignored, refused, God leaves those rejecting in their rejection?

Oh, I believe God will take into account all kinds of extenuating circumstances. Everyone will be given every benefit of the doubt. God will bend over backwards. The reach of God's mercy will be long and large.

Yet, as Jesus said in his parable of the wise and foolish maidens, at some point the door will be shut. The invitation is extended, but only for so long.

Like Moses of old pleading with God to change God's mind from time to time, I do hope the saints of the ages will try to persuade God to find some marvelous way to bring all to glory. But I do not know.

The rich man in the parable in Luke 18 wanted someone from the dead to go and warn his five brothers—perhaps to tell them that how they lived in this world mattered, and mattered eternally. As told in the parable, Abraham responded that Moses and the prophets provided adequate perspective and warning.

We may well choose to live as though it really does not matter how we live, what we think, what we believe, or what we do. We have the full freedom to live that way. We may choose to think that in the end God will, in utter benevolence, simply swing wide the gates. But according to the witness of Moses, the prophets, and Jesus, I would not count on it.

Chapter 5

Somewhere Near Woxall

ADVENT

December 18, 1994

Luke 1:39-66

This is how the text for this fourth Sunday of Advent begins:"In those days Mary set out and went with haste to a Judean town in the hill country. . . ."

What remains so disarmingly intriguing about the Christmas story is the delightful, amazing intersecting of the ordinary and the extraordinary, the mundane and the miraculous, the human and the transcendent. And wouldn't you know, the ordinary remains ordinary, while at the same time it becomes quite extraordinary.

It's like the water in baptism—it remains water, but it is more. Or the bread at communion. It tastes like bread, but it is more.

Let's watch this dynamic as this little story unfolds from the text in Luke 1. While we are watching it unfold in the story, let's let it illuminate our lives as well.

"Mary set out and went with haste to a Judean town in the hill country." Population unknown, name not mentioned, obviously a Woxall[8] kind of place. Numbers of times the Scriptures take pains to note that Jesus came from Nazareth, not so much to make the point that Jesus was from Nazareth as to make the point that Jesus was not from Jerusalem, or Rome, Athens, Alexandria.

It is in the hill country, somewhere near a Woxall, that things are stirring. And there is a stirring in the wombs of two women.

God is about to begin a new initiative. The old way has pretty well run out of steam. Kings, prophets, empires, temples, law, priests—all have come, and most have gone. The religious system has run out of creativity and vitality.

Now God will launch a new initiative; a new campaign is about to begin. But where and how?

I'm sorry. One does need to smile a bit. It begins in the pregnancies of two women somewhere near a place like Woxall.

In utter vulnerability God chooses to launch the new era. It almost staggers the imagination to think of God beginning the new age in such chancey ways—pregnancies.

There were Old Testament stories of how God had dealt dramatically in days of old: fire and brimstone on Sodom and Gomorrah; floods in the days of Noah. One of the prophets envisioned that in a little while God would shake the earth. But lo, here is God at work anew in babies kicking in wombs.

There are two. Apparently God would not risk it all with one. God chooses to send a forerunner, a herald, a preparer of the way. So Elizabeth is with child. The one who had been barren conceives.

The Woxall-like intrigue continues. Why Elizabeth, why Mary? Why not the wife of a rabbi, a leader of the Sanhedrin? Why not from a family well connected? Why not from a family that already had a name, prominence, influence, stature, credibility, experience, means? There were prominent Jewish families in Rome, as Paul found out a few decades later, as well as in Ephesus, Corinth, perhaps Athens. Why not a child from one of these more accomplished family lines? Why Mary?

We are not told. But there is a clue or two. There is in Mary a kind of openness, a receptivity. James Martin writes that "The ground of the blessing pronounced upon Mary is not performance but acceptance. Mary is blessed because she is a person of faith. She is praised not because of any special quality in her but because of her trust in the action of God."[9] And "Faith," says C. H. Dodd, "is an act which is the negation of all activity, a moment of passivity out of which the strength for action comes, because in it God acts."[10]

After Mary learned of her special situation, Luke records her comment in verse 38, "Here am I, the servant of the Lord; let it be with me according to your word." Elizabeth also commended her faith, saying, "And blessed is she who believed that there would be a fulfillment of what was spoken to her by the Lord" (Luke 1:45).

From time to time, we might need to wonder whether the Spirit might tarry with us a little more frequently if we would *do* a little less and *wait* a little more. If we were a little less filled and harried, might there be a little more space for the Spirit? Were we willing to live with a little more emptiness, might we give birth to more of the things of God?

In this Woxall-like setting in the hill country, which continued for three months according to Luke's accounting as recorded in verse 56, Luke portrays and conveys additional perspective, insight, truth, and wisdom. First, one cannot miss the fact that in this significant sequence of events, in this setting where the new era is being born, the participants are exclusively two women, Elizabeth and Mary. Zechariah is not mentioned. He is now speechless in any case. Joseph as well is not mentioned.

The focus is on Elizabeth and Mary. Now, although one cannot impose contemporary issues on the first-century text, one should look for its original significance. This text makes it clear that Mary stands on her own. She is not Joseph's wife. She is the one favored by God to be the marvelous means of God's complete self-expression in human form and flesh.

Protestants historically have been so careful to avoid the Catholic veneration of Mary that she has been given little attention and place. Luke, it appears, deliberately places her and Elizabeth center square in the new initiative of God toward humankind.

Nor is Luke yet finished. For it is from the heart and mind of Mary that Luke hears the prophetic word of what will be the effect of the one she carries in her womb.

To be sure there are other prophecies—Zechariah's mouth is opened, and he speaks profoundly. Simeon also utters special insight. But the Song of Mary resounds down through the centuries as a word and vision that cut to the very heart of the ideologies and visions that nearly all live by. Mary's song definitively turns on its head the accepted wisdom, the settled summary of the purposes of life, the way things are, the hopes and dreams that drive societies, cultures, and individuals.

You see, not only did God choose a Woxall-like place to launch the new era, not only did God select an un-prominent woman as the instrumentality of the incarnation, but that is also how things will be. Woxall-like places are where it's at in God's kingdom. Woxall-like people are the citizens of the kingdom. In the great banquet to come, Woxall-like people will be all over the place. Those who think they are where the real action is will be utterly, utterly surprised. God is up to a phenomenal reversal, and Mary puts it in the bluntest of language.

In Mary the great reversal has begun. An unknown woman surrounded by the Holy Spirit launches the new era. So certain, so clear, so sure is the evidence of this reversal that Mary's song is cast in the past tense. So certain is the biblical vision that it is told as a done deal. The language is strong and powerful:

> His mercy is for those who fear him from generation to generation. He has shown strength with his arm; he has scattered the proud in the thoughts of their hearts. He has brought down the powerful from their thrones, and lifted up the lowly; he has filled the hungry with good things, and sent the rich away empty.

Fred Craddock writes:

> Luke expresses in sharpest focus what has been called a classical statement of God's activity: the lowly are raised and the lofty are brought low. Mary sings of the God who brings down the mighty and exalts those of low degree, who fills the hungry and sends the rich away empty, and through her Luke introduces a theme prominent in both the gospel and Acts. More is involved than the social message and ministry of Jesus on behalf of the oppressed and poor. That will follow, to be sure, but there we have a characteristic of the final judgment of God in which there is complete reversal of fortunes: the powerful and rich will exchange places with the powerless and poor. And this eschatological reversal has already begun; God's choice of Mary is evidence of it.[11]

Another writer observes that "when the kingdom of God comes, all our 'kingdoms' are shown up to be the miserable fiefdoms they really are."[12]

Is it any wonder that the people of the earth revere Mary? What amazing hope she brings! The people of Woxall will be on the map; those who thought they were the center of the world will be surprised.

But now we have a problem. Here in Montgomery County, we here today, are people of wealth, power, culture, status, and position. When seen through kingdom eyes, we are on the wrong side of the tracks. We the people of privilege are on the losing end in the great judgment, the great reversal.

There is no question that in the great banquet in the age to come the great multitudes will be from the Southern Hemisphere, from the hills of Judea, from the places of the world somewhere near Woxall.

So what shall we do? Is our education, our wealth, our hard-earned position of no value? Shall we give away all and go on welfare?

A few suggestions. First, let us live by the realization that when it comes to the end of the age, what really matters is not education, position, wealth, our degrees, where we went to school, our position in the company, our bank account. None of these will cut it with St. Peter, not one whit. The things that count in this society do not count in the kingdom.

Are these of no value? Shall we not encourage education? Shall we not pursue opportunities to use our abilities? Is sloth to be encouraged? No. The issue is this: What is our position, our education, our wealth used for?

Have we turned ourselves in Mary's direction? Have we turned our lives away from the selfish focus on me and my well-being into concern for the neighbor, concern for the less fortunate? Do we see the single mother down the street as of equal value as the head of the corporation?

William Barclay tells the story of Muretus, a wandering scholar of the Middle Ages. He was poor.

> In an Italian town he took ill and was taken to a hospital for poor and homeless types. The doctors were discussing his case in Latin, never dreaming he could understand. They suggested that since he was such a worthless wanderer, they might use him for medical experiments. He looked up and answered them in their own learned tongue, "Call no man worthless for whom Christ died."[13]

Because of Mary and the vision of Mary, the church cannot and will not sit comfortably with the way society pits economic class against class. The church will not sit quietly while the rich get richer, and the poor get poorer. Someone has said that the church must be a leaven of discontent. In its life and witness the church will take up Mary's song and vision.

When Anna Quindlen wrote her final column for the editorial section of *The New York Times*, she chose not to focus on the Wall Street bankers, or the TV or movie tycoons, or the leading politicians in Washington or Albany. No, she chose to highlight the stories of persons of unusual skill and talent, persons of success in their various vocations who chose to give some of their time to a soup kitchen or to a home for prostitutes. These persons, she said, are the ones to be recognized and honored.[14] In this she understood Mary.

So the Song of Mary is about humbling the proud, bringing down the powerful, sending the rich away empty. But that Song is also about lifting up the lowly and filling the hungry with good things.

The story is about the visitation of God to people and places in the hills of Judea—Woxall-like places.

If our hearts are open, waiting, receptive, I wonder whether people in places somewhere near Woxall might also sense God's special presence and love.

Chapter 6

Mending the World

SERIES: THEMES FROM THE
MENNONITE CONFESSION OF FAITH
February 19, 1995
Ephesians 2:11-22; Matthew 5:13-16

In the family in which I grew up there were seven of us children—two girls and five boys. We lived on a farm. It took a lot
of work clothes. Our jeans, or overalls, as we called them then,
seemed to need mending regularly. The knees wore through
from handling hay bales. Every now and then the seams split.
We got caught on barbed wire fences or other places and tore
holes. On occasion we splattered battery acid and a whole cluster of little holes appeared on the jeans.

My mother was constantly amazed and at times perturbed
at the multiple ways we got holes in jeans. She patched them. She
was good at it. No matter where the tear, she found amazing
ways to repair the jeans, sometimes putting patch upon patch.

When our children were growing up, they, too, found ways
to tear jeans. My mother volunteered to mend them.

Remember when patched jeans came into style? You paid
good money for patched jeans at department stores. No reflection on the Koreans or Taiwanese or whoever made the patched
jeans, but they were no match for the artistic quality of my
mother's patched jeans. Our sons had the full admiration of their
teammates on the local ball team.

In our review in recent weeks of key themes and understandings of the faith, we have noted that while the world was

created good, the creation has been marred, besmirched, polluted. Humans have been responsible. Exercising their freedom, human beings one and all have gone their own way. The collective result is alienation, tension, greed, lust, violence, and more.

Now things are broken, torn, split, ripped, shattered.

But God the Creator still loves the world, loves it passionately. Our Scriptures speak of this God mending things. The mending began in the call of Abraham and Sarah. The descendants of Abraham and Sarah were to be a people to bless all nations. We have been blessed, and continue to be, by the Jewish people.

A further and we believe truly inaugural effort in the mending took place in Jesus. In ways we still find difficult to describe or comprehend, somehow in Jesus—in his life and ministry, death, and resurrection—reconciliation, restoration, and atonement were and are made possible..

The further mending of the world is now in large measure in the hands of the church. By its very life, the church gives witness to the mending, and by its ministry it seeks to help with the mending of the world. Our *Confession of Faith in a Mennonite Perspective* (Herald Press, 1995) talks about both aspects under the title of "The Church of Jesus Christ" and "The Church in Mission." Let's address each in. turn.

The New Testament uses many images to describe the church. All are meaningful and helpful. In our text read from Ephesians 2 you would have noticed several of these images. In verse 20 the image is that of the household of God. In verse 21 the image is that of a holy temple.

Another image which threads its way through this text and many others on the church in the New Testament is that of a new community, or here in verse 15, of a new humanity. This vision lies central to Article 8 on the church in our own *Confession of Faith in a Mennonite Perspective*. At one place the *Confession* puts it that "The church is the new community of disciples. . . ." Or again, "The church is the new society established and sustained by the Holy Spirit."[15]

We must ask, of course, What is new, different? A compelling New Testament vision is that the newness lies in the way in which the barriers of society, divisions, factions, classes, races, nationalities are broken down, overcome, transcended in the new community.

We have to place ourselves in the context of the first century to feel the power of this text in Ephesians 2. It is an understatement to suggest that there was a division between Jew and Gentile. There was in fact hatred and contempt. It went to such extremes, suggests William Barclay, that some Jews suggested that Gentiles were "created by God to be fuel for the fires of hell."[16]

There was virtually no interaction between races. If a Jew married a Gentile, the Jewish community held a funeral for the one who had crossed the racial barrier.

Gentiles were seen as far, far away from the stream of holy history. Today's text in Ephesians 2 puts this thought in the words, "aliens from the Commonwealth of Israel, and strangers to the covenant of promise, having no hope and without God in the world."

In the church of the first century, slowly, painfully, with much dispute and tension, Jews and Gentiles sat together. Paul never ceased to rejoice in and celebrate this spiritual phenomenon. The vision and the celebration pop up all over the New Testament. In Galatians, "As many of you as were baptized into Christ have clothed yourselves with Christ. There is no longer Jew or Greek, there is no longer slave or free, there is no longer male and female; for all of you are one in Christ Jesus" (Gal. 3:27-28). In 1 Corinthians we read, "For in the one Spirit we were all baptized into one body. . . . Jews or Greeks, slaves or free—we were all made to drink of one Spirit" (1 Cor. 12:13). Again in Colossians, "There is no longer Greek and Jew, circumcised and uncircumcised, barbarian, Scythian, slave and free; for Christ is all and in all" (Col. 3:11).

Thus the compelling vision persists.

But walls and barriers were not only the problem of the first century. We too have become experts in building walls, erecting barriers, fueling divisions. So in our time the world remains divided—nations, races, classes, political preferences, economic classes, educational experience, age groupings. Our society ever finds new ways to divide, separate.

The church, however, dismantles, moves, transcends, overcomes. Or it should. William Barclay tells the delightful story from World War II about French soldiers bringing the body of a dead comrade to a cemetery for burial. When the priest learned it was not certain that the dead soldier had been baptized Roman Catholic, he sadly refused burial in the cemetery. The soldiers buried their friend outside the cemetery. On returning the next day to check on the grave, they could not find it.

> They knew that it was only six feet from the fence of the burying ground, but search as they might, they could find no trace of the freshly dug soil. As they were about to leave in perplexed bewilderment, the priest came up. He told them that his heart had been troubled because of his refusal to allow the dead comrade to be buried in the church yard; so . . . early in the morning he had risen from his bed, and with his own hands *he had moved the fence* to include the body of the soldier. . . .[17]

Yes, the vision of the church as a reconciling community rings loud and clear. Would that those who feel rejected, pushed aside, not valued, could hear and feel the benediction of this text: "So then you are no longer strangers and aliens, but you are citizens with the saints and also members of the household of God."

Now I have focused largely here on one image, that of a reconciling community, a new community. Another image often used in the New Testament is that of the family of God. The vision is one of a household in which the bruises of life can be gently bandaged, hurts healed, failures acknowledged and forgiven, discouragements shared. Here in the family it is hoped that the tears can be mended.

Of course the church family here and elsewhere has not measured up to the ideal, the vision. We are so terribly human. Rather than healing, the church has—more than a few times—hurt. Rather than bandaging up the brush burns, the church has inflicted its own scrapes and bruises. The church, too, needs continuing mending.

But the vision remains. And hopefully enough of the glorious possibility is experienced so that we begin to get a feel for what can be. The music is still frequently off key, but the melody breaks in beautifully on occasion, so we practice some more.

Douglass John Hall writes that

> Because God is both creator and redeemer of the world, the world, though distorted, could still be different from what

it is. And faith hears in this 'could still be' both the permission and the command to participate in God's transforming work."[18]

And when the vision begins to take form and shape, it is a thing of beauty. Where the barriers are broken down, the fellowship is wonderful. Where the healing has taken place, we are stronger. Where the jeans have been patched, mended carefully and lovingly, it is a work of art.

John Stott writes,

> It would be hard to exaggerate the grandeur of this vision. The new society God has brought into being is nothing short of a new creation, a new human race, whose characteristic is no longer alienation, but reconciliation, no longer division and hostility, but unity and peace. This new society God rules and loves, and lives in.[19]

Through its very being then, through its very life, through what is happening in its midst, the church is witness, light, salt. We see this in Jew and Gentile at the same table, the bruised and torn lovingly nursed back to wholeness, the discouraged strengthened.

The church is a witness first and foremost by what it is. If it comes anywhere near the vision of what it can be, the church is a City on a Hill. It is a light to the world. It is the salt of the earth. Our *Confession* puts it,

> The church is called to witness to the reign of Christ by embodying Jesus' way in its own life and patterning itself after the reign of God. Thus it shows the world a sample of life under the lordship of Christ. By its life, the church is to be a city on a hill, a light to the nations, testifying to the power of the resurrection by a way of life different from the societies around it.[20]

But this is no passive assignment. The church does not just sit there. The church gets caught up in God's redeeming energy. The church gets caught up in the truth that God loves the world and would mend it. To that end, the church sees itself as an instrument in the hands of the Creator and Redeemer.

And so the powerful images of light and salt. The church is not light so it can simply see to read its own Bible (good as that is). It is light for the world. The church is not salt so that we feel good, satisfying our own taste buds. No, we are salt for the earth.

There are at least two dangers for the church, and over the years the church has succumbed to both. The first is to become so like the world that the saltiness is dissipated. Then, Jesus said, it is good for nothing. A second danger is for the church to seek so hard to preserve its saltiness that it stays in the salt shaker.

In the parable of the talents, Jesus powerfully suggested that selfish attempts to preserve what has been given will result in losing all of it. The church thrives not in a protective mode but only in a mission mode. Unless the gospel is out there in the marketplace engaging the times, it will wither. The first and foremost business of the church is not its preservation; its foremost task and opportunity is demonstration and witness.

We will not rediscover the Anabaptist vision simply by reflection on the sixteenth century (important as that first century of Anabaptism was). We rediscover the vision as we engage the people and issues of our time. The church does not exist for itself—it exists for the world. Douglass John Hall describes it as not an elite but an elect community.[21] The church has been elected for a purpose—elected to be the instrument of God's saving grace, God's healing power, God's gracious mercy to a world staggering in its own waywardness. Peter put it unequivocally in 1 Peter 2:9: "But you are a chosen race, a royal priesthood, a holy nation, God's own people, in order that you may proclaim the mighty acts of him who called you out of darkness into his marvelous light."

Gordon Kauffman writes,

> The life of the church . . . has a double reference: backward to the acts through which God has been overcoming man's autonomy and secularity, establishing a community within history which knows [God] as . . . Lord; and outward to the world still unaware of God's love and care, to whose wounds, suffering, and death she must minister in the hope and expectation that ultimately all those who presently are "no people" will come to be explicitly, and to know themselves as, "God's people."[22]

We go into the world as Jesus did—humbly, gently, without instruments of power. As we go into the midst of the enmity, amid the pains and hurts of the world, it will not be pain-free. This is a costly way. Costly in terms of time, energy, and resources. Costly in terms of misunderstanding. Costly in the sense that some of the hurts and bruises of the world must be absorbed by those who would heal and reconcile.

But what a joy, what a privilege, what a calling, what a vocation, what a challenge! As Douglass John Hall puts it,

> Creation is not a failed experiment. It has not been abandoned by the one who brought it into being. It is not given over to the processes of disintegration and death that were introduced into it by forces other than the will of its creator. It is being "mended."[23]

Can you think of anything more worthwhile than to participate in the mending? We work and we hope.

This week, surely if our eyes are open, our hearts sensitive, there will be more than a few opportunities to put in a stitch here, a stitch there, to mend this or that, to sew, to restore.

Patched jeans are beautiful jeans.

Chapter 7

An Uncommon People

SERIES: BEING ANABAPTIST IN THE TWENTY-FIRST CENTURY
April 28, 1996
Luke 6:32-36; Matthew 18:21-35

We have heard the stories of persons who have traveled to various places in Europe where everyone marvels at the magnificent cathedrals while noting that few attend church. For a good percentage of the population in England, I'm told, you will be found in church primarily on three occasions—baptism as an infant, marriage, and a funeral. The church is ceremonial.

Things are different here. Church attendance is far more frequent, the vast majority believe in God, prayer is on the way back. But there is reason for concern. One must ask, How deep does faith and belief really cut into people's lives? Or (as I tried to ask the question last week), which story, which ideology, really shapes us?

The gods of this world are real and powerful. We do not live in a climate of neutrality in which a little dose of spirituality a few times a year wins the day. The dominant worldview of materialism, militarism, and self-fulfillment pushes and presses, invites and entices, every day in multiple ways.

If we choose to live by the story of the faith, if the witness of Abraham and Sarah, Miriam and Moses, Jeremiah and Isaiah, Mary and Joseph, and particularly Jesus is to have its way with us, what consequences will there be? In the question of the gospel song, "Can one tell you've been with Jesus, can they by your life and mine?"

It has been a persistent perspective of our faith tradition that faith has outcomes, that salvation is much more than a spiritual transaction in the inner recesses of the soul. Our tradition has expected that when one is washed in the waters of baptism and rises up in newness of resurrection life, there is outward evidence. The book of James argues vigorously that deeds are the expression of faith. Stanley Hauerwas writes that "any community . . . is known and should be judged by the kind of people it develops."[24]

Admittedly, as a Mennonite people we have a troubled past in relation to these matters. So traumatic has been the experience of some a generation or two back and sometimes still today that feelings still emerge. So I have stayed away from words so intertwined with wounds—a peculiar people, nonconformity, a disciplined church. Memory, stories, and mythology of heavy-handed authority and indoctrination have so traumatized us as a church that Sara Wenger Shenk writes, "With a sense of inferiority and failure, many of us have acquired a distaste for the pungent flavor of our own history and our own people; we are looking for a generic menu served up to individual preference."[25]

For those of us who share Shenk's experience, our distaste for nonconformity and our embarrassment about being different is coupled with a powerful mood of our time that hawks individual preference as though each individual is naturally endowed with unlimited moral wisdom. So in the name of encouraging our children to develop their special individuality, or to experience the broad range of human experience, we permit them to explore this or that as if each option is of equal value. Then, when the dominant values of this society have their full play and full grip on our children, we express disappointment that the values we cherish have not been affirmed.

The recent generation of parents in American society has been so careful not to control the next generation. Freedom has been the watchword. And now, when many are addicted to various substances, struggling to pay off credit card debts, and unable to find enduring loving relationships, this society must honestly ask itself about freedom and where true freedom lies.

It is our understanding that the story of the faith, the vision of the kingdom, has shaping power and expectation. I shall not deal with all aspects of this now. For today, I simply wish to contend that the story of the faith, if heard, forms and shapes thinking and behavior—profoundly, distinctively, markedly, pointedly, visibly.

So as to slip by all the accumulated prejudices of our own history, and our society's bias against religious conviction, I use the softest language I can think of and speak of "an uncommon people." Today I wish to point out what might be characterized as dispositions or habits of the heart through which the faith forms an uncommon people.

Four themes seem to me germane to biblical faith. (These themes are implicit, if not always explicit, in the Anabaptist tradition). Further, I suggest that these themes are urgent in our time and that, if lived and expressed, they will set us off from the dispositions of our society—making us uncommon.

Turning to the first theme, a recurring and significant part of the biblical story is the way in which strangers are welcomed. The story has two sub-themes. One is that God welcomes the stranger. Abraham was told and Israel rehearsed the story that Abraham was a wandering pilgrim until God called. Paul reminds us in Romans that all of us have been strangers, all of us have been outsiders, and that it was while we were yet sinners Christ died for us.

On the other hand, the biblical story teaches us that *we* are to welcome strangers. Lo and behold, Abraham and Sarah through welcoming strangers unwittingly provided hospitality to representatives of God.

A prominent parable of Jesus is that of the Good Samaritan. And in the New Testament church the great vision of the church begins to find fulfillment when the Gentiles are welcomed.

A prominent mark of the church, a sign of an uncommon people, is when the strangers, the outcasts, the rejected are welcomed.

Prejudice is so deep in our time and going deeper. The road to faithfulness is to deliberately think, Who are the strangers in our midst? The neglected? The less valued? Who are those by the side of the road? Then we are invited to welcome such strangers, such neglected ones, such wounded ones.

Turning to the second theme, many in our society say they believe in life after death. Everybody loves Easter. The tomb is not the end, all shout and sing. But too often we live as though this is it. No, the story of the faith is that the saga of life is not limited to three score and ten. Thus we do not need to live so feverishly, as if all experiences must be squeezed into this life.

We do not have to fix everything. We do not need to even every score. We do not need to judge every incident. Things will be rightly judged and made fair and square eventually.

There will be time to experience joy and delight. If there is only this life, then Kody Shore, beloved child now gone from our midst, was hopelessly cheated. We still wish he could have had so much more of this life. But the grief is softened through faith that there is more life to come.

A people of faith live with conspicuous contentment, for whatever this life yields or does not yield, there is infinitely more to come. That kind of life is uncommon in this society.

A third theme: A pervasive cynicism stalks the land. Politicians are assumed to be self-serving. People on welfare cheat. Business people exploit. The cynicism is all the deeper because we have come to realize that technology and human intellect and ingenuity will not bring us safely home.

Our faith story does not gloss over failure. Indeed the story describes human evil and human sin pointedly and emphatically and has no notion that better education or better socialization will solve the human dilemma.

But central to our story is the belief, the faith, that there can be change, renewal, redirection, new creation. Thus we live holding out the marvelous possibility that enemies can become friends, that the broken can be healed, that conflict can be resolved, that destructive habits can be overcome, that the oppressed can be liberated, that the weak can become strong, that those bogged down can rise with energy and vision.

We refuse to believe that the universe is self-contained, that there is no new source of spiritual energy. Love and grace are not depleted. They are in boundless supply. The God whom we serve is not a God of past deeds, limited to wonders of old.

So we live, work, pray in faith, and hope that persons near and far can grow and change. Perhaps more importantly, we live and work—and pray that *we* can grow and change.

Fourth, an uncommon people will initiate steps toward forgiveness, which is to be pursued rather than revenge. Peter wondered how often must one forgive—up to seven times? No, Jesus said, much more. Seventy times seven.

Now the reference of seventy times seven goes all the way back to Genesis 4. Here the descendants of Cain found new ways to repeat the violence of Cain. One Lamech boasted to his wives that he had avenged the wrong of someone wounding him. Listen to him boast:

> "Lamech said to his wives: Adah and Zillah, hear my voice;
> you wives of Lamech, listen to what I say:
> I have killed a man for wounding me,
> a young man for striking me.
> If Cain is avenged sevenfold,
> truly Lamech seventy-seven fold."

The earth is full of the spirit of revenge. A minority in our society feel they have been deprived. Their resentment grows. They steal, even kill. The newspapers recount the details. Then society seeks its revenge. Prison terms are lengthened. The death penalty is back. The trials of criminals are reported in full detail. And now people can witness the inflicting of the lethal injections. The spirit of revenge multiplies.

The uncommon people, if wronged, seek not revenge but reconciliation. Fred Craddock writes:

> They are to take the initiative, but not by responding in kind, or by playing dead, or whining. They are not to react but to act according to the kingdom principles of love, forgiveness, and generosity. Such behavior is not a covert strategy for a soft kill ("Whip them with kindness"), but is a pursuit of that life one learns from God who does not reciprocate but who is kind even to the ungrateful and the selfish.[26]

At every level of our lives, in all of our relationships, we have the privilege, the possibility of responding to slights, offenses, wrongs, by moving toward understanding and forgiveness. Or we can retaliate. It is uncommon to forgive.

Can they tell we've been with Jesus, can they by your life and mine? How deep has the faith penetrated our lives?

Testimonies of being born again, spiritual enthusiasm on Sundays, and pious language are fine. But how does the faith express itself by mid-week in the ebb and flow of life? How much difference is there in the ways you and I react to the daily slights, frustrations, disappointments, as compared with others who make little claim of Christian faith?

And where are the people who really cut across the grain of society's prejudices, faithlessness, short-sightedness? Are we making progress toward becoming "Children of the Most High; for he is kind to the ungrateful and the wicked"? Are we merciful, just as our Father is merciful?

Or we can ask the question in Paul's words in Philippians. Is the mind of Christ being formed in us? Or in Galatians, where Paul writes, "My little children, for whom I am again in the pain of childbirth until Christ is formed in you. . ." (Gal. 4:19). We are given the high designation of being called the body of Christ. Are there signs that we have taken on his likeness?

Chapter 8

No Supplements Needed

SERIES: THE JESUS OF HISTORY AND THE CHRIST OF FAITH
May 11, 1997
Colossians 2:6-19

Do you ever walk the aisles of the drugstore? You can get an education moseying around there. One learns, for example, that there are more ailments than one may have imagined. I never knew so many things could go wrong with your stomach.

And the solutions for colds and flu are wonderful. There are daytime remedies, nighttime solutions, some that may cause drowsiness—I do not know whether that might happen in the day or at night. And everything is in such small print it convinces you something is happening to your eyesight.

So you go to the vitamin section. I'm impressed by that section; it's more hopeful. Whereas many other sections are trying to fix something wrong with you, the vitamin section holds promise. Vitamins point to the future.

The options are amazing—Spectrum, Centrum, Multi. Just hang around the vitamin section a bit, and you'll almost feel your bones getting stronger and your liver kicking in.

This is a good time to live. Everything is Extra Strength. Plus. New and Improved Version Two. I pity our grandparents' generation. They had to live when everything was regular. Can you imagine what it was like to have a headache and have no double-fast, double-action extra-strength Anacin?

You can learn a lot in a drugstore.

I doubt if the Colossians had these super drugstores, but what they did have was a whole variety of extra-strength, plus, value-added, spiritual supplements. We are not told exactly what all these extra sources for spiritual vitality were, but we can read between the lines and glimpse the spiritual vitamins available to them. In the text read we find several of these mentioned.

The Colossians were not convinced that the faith as presented to them had enough zest, power, intellectual sophistication, spiritual discipline. So they made their way up and down the aisles of the religious drugstore for added potions to mix in.

Some figured a little worship of angels would not hurt, as noted in verse 18. Some thought paying attention to the movement of the stars held possibilities. Apparently, just as Nancy Reagan would not let President Reagan travel on certain days, these Colossians figured that the movement of the stars and planets figured into their well-being.

Others chose a dietary route. What they did or did not eat could somehow enhance their spiritual well-being. Some called for the reassertion of observances of the Jewish holy days. And some figured the old practice of circumcision would not be a bad idea.

Paul was not impressed by this multi-vitamin approach. This value-added effort left Paul troubled. He saw all kinds of problems in the Colossian efforts to mix and match a variety of religious practices, religious disciplines, self-help efforts, and novel philosophies.

Paul addresses the inadequacies of the Colossian multi-vitamin approach. In verse 8 he calls into question the various philosophies, human traditions, and the so-called spirit world hovering between earth and heaven. In verse 10, Paul intimates that the old practice of circumcision is far too superficial. In verse 18 he argues that to worship angels is to worship the created rather than the Creator. In the few verses that follow our text, Paul continues his serious questioning of various disciplines or regulations, suggesting that these self-help efforts appear to be ways of piety and humility but really fail to transcend self-focus.

What really seems to trouble Paul is that all these rules, self-improvement efforts, intellectual exercises, and dabbling miss that which yields life, that which holds the great promise, that which brings fullness—namely Christ. The poor Colossians! They wanted to expand their hearts and minds, so they went up and down the spiritual drugstore aisles. Others suggested that all these new ideas were the wrong direction; needed were the old laws, the old commandments, the practices of yesteryear. But Paul would say that neither the newer extra-strength Bufferin or the old liniment would remove the aches and pains of the soul. Paul pled for them to turn anew and only to Christ Jesus the Lord.

For Jesus the Lord is the source of fullness. "For in him the whole fullness of deity dwells bodily, and you have come to fullness in him. . ." (vv. 9-10). Further, these self-help efforts to check bodily temptations are snipping at the edges—for in baptism you have been buried with Christ and the record of sin has been erased. Further, in baptism you have been raised by the power of God. Why occupy your minds with angels when the Spirit of Christ is present? Why be ruled by the ideologies and powers and fears of this world? They have been exposed by Christ as being penultimate and transitory.

Happily we are far from the first century with its strange notions. Surely we are free of trying to supplement Christian faith with additional religious dimensions. We can be relieved: There is no tendency in our time to mix with the faith other human ideologies, philosophies, rules, regulations. In our time there is no fusing of contemporary thought movements with the Christian faith.

I wish. But we too need to be alerted to various doctrines, ideologies, human efforts that compete with Christ. Let me explore several possibilities.

I wonder in what ways pervasive ideologies of the modern era have restricted or competed with the full message of the faith. Could it be that confidence in technology has misplaced our confidence and hope in God? Did we too easily assume that modern science and human ingenuity would bring us collectively and individually to fullness of life? Yet that assumption now seems misplaced. We are past the time when there was confidence that our problems could be fixed by human invention. The age of anxiety has settled in.

Has our individualism, the freedom of the individual, yielded fullness of life? That is, after all, the great Western ideal. Each to her or his own, uninhibited by the expectations or encumbrances of others. You have freedom to do as you wish, just give me the same. Some speak of their own spirituality. That kind of individualism has not brought home peace and happiness—but loneliness and fear.

Surely wealth brings security and happiness. Prosperity, health, happiness have in fact been promised by some interpreters of the faith. But a strange thing happens. The more wealthy we become, the more insecure we become. The more goods we have in our homes, the more we worry about the locks. The more we have invested in stocks, the more we read the *Wall Street Journal* and worry whether the market goes up or down. Neither poverty nor wealth brings peace of mind or heart.

We often comment on how generous are those who have little. Why? They are not nearly as tied to goods. They live with a much less protective mentality.

In our spiritual search, many of us have tried a variety of spiritual journeys. At times I wonder whether all these self-help efforts really help or hinder our openness to the full work of Christ. Do they go far enough? Everywhere you turn in the Western Christian world there are suggestions for this effort and that—keys to successful living, seven steps to happiness, how to overcome your addictions, how to find a deeper relationship with God. Do these spiritual disciplines really open our lives to God, or might these just be efforts to increase our piety? Even prayer can be self-serving; rather than openness to God, it can become an effort to enlist God on our side or to bless our self-centered desires.

In our counseling and therapy sessions are we simply trying to come to accept who we are? Or is there openness to confess and acknowledge that we need more than what we are, that we are fundamentally off course? Are we buying various vitamins, trying to strengthen our lives with a variety of quasi-religious ingredients, while neglecting the source of life in Christ?

Have we really considered what is offered in Christ Jesus our Lord? Forgiveness of sins. Release from enslavement to ourselves or trying to do good on our own power. Resurrection power to live anew. The very fellowship of Christ and his body. The freedom that comes from wanting to do the right and good so that law and legalism are fully transcended. Victory from the powers of this world. We are fighting the demons of our lives with antidotes that are too weak. We fail to realize that on the cross Jesus stripped these controlling forces of their power.

Why do we stay with this confusing combination of dabbling in the ways of the faith yet stocking up on various spiritual vitamins? My hunch is that we get about halfway into the waters of the faith. But we never detach ourselves fully from the fears and anxieties of this age, so we never fully feel the power of faith to sustain us.

In the inaugural address at the inauguration of Richard Detweiler some years ago at Eastern Mennonite College, J. Lawrence Burkholder suggested that if one does not fully enter into the task, in this case being college president, a miserable experience is guaranteed. When we get close to the faith, it can look like a combination of do this and do that. It can look like something imposed—a weight. But if we get fully into the resources of God we find that the fruits of the spirit are love, joy, peace, patience, kindness, generosity, gentleness, self-control. That does not sound like restricting legalism to me. Rather, it is marvelous freedom.

This mix-and-match approach to the faith is a terribly poor substitute for the real thing. Paul writes: "As you therefore have received Christ Jesus the Lord, continue to live your lives in him, rooted and built up in him and established in the faith, just as you were taught, abounding in thanksgiving."

Chapter 9

"Things That Make for Peace"

July 6, 1997
Luke 19:41-42; Matthew 5:38-48

L et me tell you about Jenny—a retired teacher in this area. Jenny never gives up. She is fully convinced that the ways of violence need not have the upper hand. She is further convinced that there are a host of creative possibilities in peacemaking.

A number of years back Jenny, along with several others in the community, decided that not all the Russians were our enemies if we could only get to know some personally. So a Sister City arrangement was made between Boyertown and Bogodukhov in the Ukraine. Three guests came to visit Boyertown— the mayor of the city and two women, both officials in the local communist party.

We hosted these folks in our homes. In our own home the two women cooked for us and other friends a delightful Ukrainian meal. We still receive regular greetings from Nadia.

Some time ago Jenny was troubled by the fact that elementary and high school children tended at times to get into little skirmishes and even fights on the way to school and at school. Jenny's idea was that it is more difficult to get angry at other schoolmates if you know their names. So she helped launch a program whereby all the children on a school bus would learn to know the names of all the others on the bus. She enlisted the drivers of the school buses and the school principals in her program. It works. Where the children know each other by name the skirmishes have lessened considerably.

Violence and hatred continue as a major problem in our society at every level. The stories of conflict seem to be increasing, and the spirit of vengeance appears to be flourishing.

Bumper stickers are not the full measure of a society's spirit, but the tone of some we see and other expressions are troublesome. "Revenge is sweet" some would suggest. An argument for capital punishment is that it helps families and friends of victims to get past their anger when they know the perpetrator of the violence has been executed. The vengeful spirit of Cain in the early epoch of the human family continues to flourish.

Is there anything to be done? Does the Christian church have any response? Are any creative contributions possible?

For Mennonites, peace in all dimensions of life has been an important aspect of understanding the gospel. Traditionally we have termed our position versus violence as "nonresistant." At a minimum, this meant that we would not add to the violence. Thus we have taught non-participation in warfare.

While the position of nonresistance is commendable, it does not fully respond to the call of Jesus to be peacemakers. The God we serve has not chosen a posture of noninvolvement. Our text from Matthew 5:9 suggests that those who take up the task of peacemaking have begun to take on the character of God. Drawing on the text read from Matthew 5:38-48, let me suggest three peacemaking possibilities, and then I'll add two more suggestions.

First, the response of nonresistance can well be more than noninvolvement. Jesus amplified the perspective of not reacting to violence when he added that one should be willing to absorb a second blow or walk an extra mile.

Involved here is not necessarily a strategy of trying to melt the heart of the opponent. To be sure, Paul suggests (Rom. 12) that we should try to overcome evil with good. Perhaps that is what is implied here, but the angry personalities generally do not change quickly.

The suggestion here is that one should not give in to the spirit of the perpetrator of violence small or large. By turning the other cheek, and by going the second mile, one is fully exercising one's freedom; one is not giving over to a similar spirit of the opponent. I like the response of someone who said, after being struck by an angry person, "I see that words fail you."

In a vengeful response to hatred and violence, one can become so quickly like the one who strikes. Again and again one can see that, as vengeance builds on vengeance, the perpetrator and victim soon become indistinguishable. In a vengeful response one becomes like the enemy.

A second initiative in peacemaking is suggested in Matthew 5:44. The peacemaker is to love the enemy. No easy task.

Now I do not know that Jesus was calling for some immediate warm, tender feelings toward the enemy. Called for here is love as an act—love as something one does. The call is to undertake initiatives similar to those done by the God who sends rain on the friend and foe alike. Here the encouragement is that some act or deed of kindness be extended to those who have done us ill.

The vision here is simply to mirror, in some ways, however imperfectly, the character of God. That is how God-likeness is exhibited. That is how it is seen that there is some resemblance that the Christian is of the family of God. To become a son or daughter of God is to participate in the divine nature by reflecting God's unconditional love for all made in God's image.

A third aspect of peacemaking spoken to in this text is that of prayer. The disciple is enjoined to pray for the opponent, the one who persecutes. Now it is immediately clear what then happens. One can hardly pray for another and simultaneously wish that person ill. To pray for another is to begin to look at the other from God's point of view. One begins to get in touch with the pains, sorrows, and disappointments of the other. One begins to imagine the sufferings of the other. Not all disagreements will evaporate immediately, but the person prayed for becomes multi-dimensional; the humanness of the opponent comes into view.

Two additional "things that make for peace" are not directly touched on in these texts but are exhibited in the life of Jesus and the witness of the early church. The first seems initially contrary to peacemaking. It is the call to protest. Indeed, this seems at first thought to be actually conflict-making.

But in reflecting on the example of Jesus, one cannot avoid the realization that he protested. He protested evil. He protested the teachings of the scribes and Pharisees. He protested the injustice of the tax collectors. He protested when children were ignored. He protested the practices in the temple. He protested when the poor were neglected.

I wonder if the church has raised its voice sufficiently against a variety of evils of our time. Is there sufficient protest against capital punishment? Has the church raised its voice adequately against those who care too little for the well-being of the environment? Have we spoken up for the concerns of the poor?

Finally, the call to peacemaking is the call to preach. At least three times in Scripture appears the poetic imagery of "how beautiful are the feet of those who preach the message of peace."

There are two aspects of this. First, violence does not work as well as the proponents of violence think. This society is convinced that violence will fix things. The spirit of Cain simply yields more of the spirit of Cain.

The power of violence is an illusionary power. In the book of Revelation it is seen as the illusionary power of the beast. The Christian is called on to expose or unmask this power.

Second, there is the invitation to alert all who would hear that conflict and violence need not have the upper hand. Hatred and vengeance need not rule the human heart. The great message of the Christian faith is a message of grace, mercy, forgiveness. Hearts can be changed, attitudes turned around. The headlines of the events of our world need not always be those of violence.

Teilhard de Chardin wrote that

> The day will come, after harnessing space, the winds, the tides, and gravitation, we shall harness for God the energies of love. And, on that day, for the second time in the history of the world, we shall have discovered fire.[27]

Chapter 10

Creatures, Wheels, Glory

SERIES: TEXTS FROM JEREMIAH AND EZEKIEL
January 4, 1998
Ezekiel 1

Her name was Ruby Bridges. If I have the story right, it was in the early 1960s. Ruby was six when she was selected to be the first African-American, or as the term was then, the first Negro student to attend what had been an all-white elementary school in Louisiana.

The white folks were adamantly opposed. So opposed that federal marshals were called in to protect Ruby as she made her way to school.

Every morning Ruby walked calmly, quietly, toward the school while the community white folks protested, shouted, threatened. Tensions were high, feelings deep, hatred evident on faces and in words. But Ruby entered the school quietly, calmly, seemingly fully in control.

People from around the country, as they watched on TV the events unfolding, began to marvel at how a six-year-old child could face turmoil, hatred, threats, and potential violence with such strength and steadiness. Ruby's parents were not trained in meeting conflict. They were common folk, poor, just a simple Louisiana family.

One day Ruby was walking through the crowd, once again facing all the racial epithets and the threats, when those close to her saw her lips move. They thought she was saying something. That further incited their anger.

When she got into class that day, she was asked what she had said as she had approached the school. Ruby replied that she had not spoken. They pressed her further, and told her that persons had seen her lips move. No, she said, she had not spoken. But they insisted that she must have; her lips moved like she was speaking.

Well, Ruby explained, every day before she left home she said a prayer. But this morning she had forgotten to say the prayer, so she prayed it on the way to school. They pressed her more and asked what the prayer was. She replied, "Father, forgive them for they know not what they do."[28]

Robert Coles, Professor of Psychiatry at Harvard Medical School, has studied children. Of particular interest to Coles has been the spiritual and moral development of children. Two of his recent books carry the titles of *The Spiritual Life of Children* and *The Moral Intelligence of Children*. Coles was of course intrigued by Ruby Bridges. What was it that kept her steady, calm and collected amid this most threatening situation?

Coles concluded that it was the stories she had heard at church and home that prepared her to meet this hostile environment. In church and at home, Ruby had been provided with a moral framework and character that served her unusually well.

The biblical story provides a story, a language, images and symbols that are sufficiently deep and broad, sufficiently coherent, sufficiently strong that if we learn them, if we absorb them, we can face life in confidence and hope.

Our task here is to tell the story, to ponder it, to let the themes of the story and the God of the story stir our thoughts and imagination, to let it soak deep into our souls, to let it shape the way we define our lives, and to give definition to our responses to the situations we face in life.

The story we believe is big enough. It deals with the big questions—life and death, judgment and grace, failure and salvation. The rooms of the biblical story are large enough to live in. And no matter how wavering or meandering our walk, the biblical story provides a path to meaning and joy to which we can return.

Now we cannot get the whole biblical story in all its power, breadth, depth in ten easy lessons. There is no *Reader's Digest* condensed version that successfully packages the story in a neat form that we can read and absorb on a lunch break. It takes time to absorb it all. The story is multi-dimensional—you must view it from different angles. It takes on deeper meaning from the varied experiences of life.

Beginning this Sunday, we want to launch into a series of Sundays in which we will turn to a portion of the Older Testament to let that segment of Scripture have its say to us. During these Sundays we are not coming to the Scriptures with this or that question or problem and asking what the Scripture says about our issue. Rather, we'll try to let the Scripture speak what it has to say.

We will turn first to the prophet Ezekiel. You might find this a strange choice. Ezekiel is long and repetitious. Worse yet, Ezekiel we would say is a little off the wall, at times quite strange, even bizarre. At places we can hardly figure out what Ezekiel was meaning to say. So why Ezekiel?

Well, the book is in the Bible. I'm rather sure few of you have read it in the last year or two. Yet the people of faith thought it important—they included it in our collection of sacred writings.

Ezekiel stirs the imagination, and I hope will stir our spiritual blood a little. Ezekiel stretches the religious mind. The prophet spoke in one of the most creative eras of the development of the Judeo-Christian faith.

What we hope to accomplish in these weeks is to fill our souls a little with the kind of goods that kept Ruby Bridges calm and collected. We want to fill our spiritual reservoirs with some of the big themes, the rich imagination of Scripture. We want to plant in our minds "texts that linger, words that explode," to use a phrase from Walter Brueggemann.[29]

A word about Ezekiel and the times in which he spoke. Actually, we know little about who this person was. We are told in 1:3 that he was the son of Buzi and was of the priestly class of Israel. That is about it. Anything more we must come by through reading between the lines.

Of the times during which Ezekiel prophesied or spoke we know much more. They were troubled times, troubled with a capital "T"! Ezekiel, the prophet/priest, was not speaking from the temple in Jerusalem but in the land of Babylon, miles away from Jerusalem. He was by the river Chebar in an area now part of Iraq.

The time when Ezekiel began to speak was 593 BC. He had been among the first group of refugees to be driven from Jerusalem and taken to Babylon. Permit a brief sketch of the political situation of Ezekiel's time. For decades prior to his being taken to Babylon, the southern section of Israel, referred to in the Scriptures as the land of Judah, was caught amid tremendous power struggles between three empires—the Egyptian, Assyrian, and Babylonian.

Judah, seeking to survive, would try to align itself with one or the other empire, only to find itself aligned with the empire about to be defeated by the other. Political advisers abounded in Jerusalem, giving totally conflicting advice. Prophets of all kinds threw in their ten cents. These were the days of Jeremiah, when all kinds of prophets declared that God would protect Jerusalem, the city of God, and that the temple could not be destroyed because it was the place where God dwelt. Jeremiah rose to declare that these prophecies were wrong, not helpful, and worse. Few listened, and Jeremiah was, to say the least, somewhere below the bottom of the popularity charts.

At the end of this power struggle, the Babylonian Empire won out. Judah was taken captive. The first wave of deportation had taken place a few years before Ezekiel began to prophecy. During the time of his prophesying, twenty-two years from 593 to 571 BC, the puppet king in Judah had the crazy notion to stage some kind of rebellion against Babylon. That so angered the Babylonian rulers that in 586 BC they ravaged the city of Jerusalem, including the temple.

What makes the story all the more riveting is that the destruction of Jerusalem and particularly the temple was then not only a political crisis but also a profoundly religious one. For the people of faith had been under the clear impression that God had promised to protect and preserve his people, and the temple was the place of God's earthly dwelling. How could God permit Jerusalem to fall and the temple to be destroyed? Was God not able? Was God weak? Did God not keep promises? Were the Babylonian gods after all to be acknowledged? Worshiped?

In this profound crisis of faith, Ezekiel rose to speak. And in the reformulation of the faith, Ezekiel is one of three major prophets. I spoke of the role of Jeremiah. Ezekiel follows him.

And after Ezekiel come the words of the prophet in the second part of the book of Isaiah, often referred to as second Isaiah.

So along the river Chebar, among a group of refugees, Ezekiel sees a vision. It is a strange one, and we cannot catch all the symbolism and its meaning. But the essential themes seem clear.

One aspect of the vision is the quartet of four creatures, with their four faces. The appearances are of a man, an ox, an eagle, and a lion. These represent the major areas of creation—man, the highest of creation; the lion, the king of wild beasts; the ox, the strongest of domesticated animals; and the eagle, who rules the air. In the vision these were borne above the earth, perhaps symbolizing that all of nature is under God's domain.

Most easily understood is the imagery of the wheels. The chariot is borne by an amazing combination of them. They are of such a configuration that whatever contains the four creatures can move in any direction. It is entirely mobile—it can move up, down, sideways, straight, or in any combination. It is certainly not fixed or situated at one place.

Those who had in their minds that God was confined to one place—the temple in Jerusalem—would see in the vision the truth that the dwelling place of God can move in every direction—north, south, east, west. God was anything but stationary. They had thought God had dwelt singularly in the temple in Jerusalem.

The vision moves on to declare some of the glory and grandeur of the presence and dwelling of God. And here Ezekiel tries his best, but there was inadequate language to describe what he saw. Words fall short. Notice in verses 26 and following that what we have are repeated similes: phrases of "something like," "appearance like," "likeness," "something that seemed like," "something that looked like. . . ."

Such was the grandeur of God. Those who had thought that the only place of God's dwelling was back in Jerusalem had to be stirred by the vision of Ezekiel. For even along the river Chebar, in the refugee camp far from home, there, too, Ezekiel saw the glory and grandeur of the God of Israel—a glory and grandeur that defied description.

The refugees had also feared that perhaps God was captive in Jerusalem, held prisoner in the temple. Ezekiel saw God gloriously present along the river Chebar, moving in time and space at will. The refugees along that foreign river thought they were abandoned, alone. The events of history, they thought, moved faster than God. But Ezekiel saw a wheel.

The God of Abraham and Sarah, the God of our Lord Jesus Christ, is never the prisoner of the events of this world. The wheels of his chariot move whatever way God chooses to move.

Chapter 11

Everything Lives Where the Water Goes

SERIES: TEXTS FROM JEREMIAH AND EZEKIEL
February 22, 1998
Ezekiel 47:1-12

A mid difficult and chaotic times, every now and then someone rises to proclaim a vision, a dream. And the dream or vision is of such power and imagination that the moment is transformed, the future is envisioned, and hope is reborn.

One thinks of President Lincoln's Gettysburg address: "Four
score and seven years ago our fathers brought forth on this con-
tinent, a new nation, conceived in Liberty, and dedicated to the
proposition that all men are created equal."

Or one recalls the address of President John F. Kennedy at
the American University, where the president moved beyond
the rhetoric of the Cold War and the world seemed less threatening and dark.

Some of us will recall the "I Have a Dream" speech of Martin
Luther King Jr. Delivered from the steps of the Lincoln Memorial
in Washington, D.C., in August 1963, amid the civil rights movement. One can still hear King's voice rising:

> I have a dream that one day on the red hills of Georgia, the
> sons of former slaves and the sons of former slave owners
> will be able to sit together at a table of brotherhood.
>
> I have a dream that my four children will one day live
> in a nation where they will not be judged by the color of

their skin but by the content of their character.
I have a dream today.

The cadences of this great American orator still ring in our ears.

For several years along the banks of the Chebar River in Babylon, the prophet Ezekiel had delivered speeches of power, speeches of rich imagery, speeches of startling imagination. But these were not speeches that stirred hope, that created a future. Rather they were repetitive speeches of judgment, woe, despair, lament, sorrow, pain. The hammer of Ezekiel's words pounded relentlessly upon the ears of the exiles in Babylon by the river.

But then in the twenty-fifth year of the exile, Ezekiel's speeches turned. And as dramatic as Ezekiel had been in condemnation, now his language soared with images of hope. To the exiles hunkered down in Babylon, Ezekiel came with wonderful images of a rebuilt temple, a restored Jerusalem pictured brilliantly in words. Can you imagine how this must have stirred the hearts of those hopeless exiles by the river!

In 1965-1966 Ellen and I lived in the heart of Texas. Now one may have nothing against Texas, but in that flat land, in the 100-degree heat, steeped in the ethos of the Wild West, amid a kind of religious paranoia, amid a racially segregated community, one could easily dream of the hills of Pennsylvania.

It is in Chapter 40 that Ezekiel begins to relate his vision of a restored Jerusalem and a new temple. The vision is exceptionally detailed. From chapters 40-43 on, everything is described minutely. We are told the size of each gate, the size of vestibules, the number of windows, the number of steps from this court to the next, the inner court, the outer court—it goes on and on, the thickness of walls, the carvings on the walls—one wearies in reading it. Why all the detail?

Have you ever been away from home for a long time? When you have been away for a long time, any and all news is important. There is no detail that is uninteresting. I can imagine that the exiles along the river listened eagerly, attentively to every little detail of Ezekiel's visions.

In chapter 47 in the text we have read today, Ezekiel continues with an additional aspect of these visions of the New Temple. Let's see if we can feel a bit of the power of this vision as it may have felt to the exiles in Babylon.

Ezekiel sees water flowing from the temple. In the arid lands of the Middle East, water is always a rich image. Water—there never is enough of it from the day of Israel in the wilderness to today with the plight of the Palestinians on the West Bank. Water is always in short supply.

And here, in the vision, lo and behold the water increases. It gets deeper. There is more symbolism: as it flows, the river enlarges dramatically. At 1,000 cubits or nearly 600 yards, it is ankle deep. Then measured at another 1,000 cubits, it is knee deep. And another 1,000 cubits, waist deep. Can you believe it, at another 1,000 cubits one loses one's footing, one can only swim in it, and the current is so strong that one can not cross the river.

In Ezekiel's vision the river ran to the east down to the Arabah. This is a pronounced geological depression that runs north and south from modern Lebanon in the north to the Gulf of Aqaba in the south. It is a dry and barren region. Here in the vision, as the river flows the arid land becomes green and trees grow along the banks.

As the river continues, it enters the sea. The exiles knew this sea—the Dead Sea. It lies 1,300 feet below the level of the Mediterranean Sea to the west. The Dead Sea carries its name with reason. It is the pits. It has no outlet. The water is stagnant, salty, brackish—we would say polluted. It does not sustain life. In fact it is entirely inhospitable to life.

But in Ezekiel's vision, the stagnant waters become fresh. And the algae and the amoebae and the little minnows grow, the bigger fish too live and thrive. On both sides of the sea, nets are spread for fishing, and the catch is big enough to make stories. One's imagination runs even to today, as one dreams of when Jew and Palestinian could both fish, when Jew and Palestinian could both live on the land, when Jew, Muslim, and Christian could all worship in Jerusalem.

But back to Ezekiel's vision. Everywhere the river goes, life springs up. On both banks grow fruit trees—so productive that fruit can be gathered every month. And the leaves of the trees have medicinal value that brings healing.

Ezekiel, Ezekiel, you get carried away! The vision is too grand, too ideal, too far removed.

But can you imagine how this vision stirred the exiles, quickened the spirit, renewed hope, reinvigorated those given to despair? One can well imagine that under the spell of this vision, the exiles might have found somewhere in the back of their tents their old musical instruments, and that they might have sung the songs of Jerusalem with new lyrics and harmonies.

Well, we are not exiles in refugee camps by the river Chebar. Perhaps this wonderful vision has its place only in the record of the Old Testament. Perhaps. But then again, in part we, too, are a little bit in exile, amid a culture in which we dare not be fully comfortable. We, too, are never quite at home. We, too, know from time to time the aridity of life and stagnant waters. So let us ponder the text a little as a word also to us. Let me note several ways that this vision might also enrich our experience.

A river that grows wider and deeper has got to grasp our attention. How many times have we latched onto this or that self-help movement? How many how-to books have we bought? How many seminars have we attended which at best helped a little and at worst fizzled out a week or month or two later?

Or one can think in relation to religious circles how many renewal movements, revival times holding much promise, come and go with plenty of buildup. But after a time, they dry up or yield but a trickle, leaving people a little more helpless, a little more hopeless, a little more cynical.

What we long for is the spiritual journey that deepens as it goes. What catches our imagination are brothers and sisters in Christ whose depth of spirit, whose graciousness of heart, whose courage deepens year upon year.

What we long for is when the little mustard seed grows into a mighty tree, where the seven loaves and two fish yield twelve bushels left over. These are the ways of God. Why do we spend money for that which is not bread and does not satisfy? Why do we go after streams that peter out quickly?

Left to ourselves, the river of our life eventually ends in its own Dead Sea. Every life has its difficulties, its hurts, its bruises, its misunderstandings, its tensions and conflicts. Without the river of God's grace, these little hurts and bruises accumulate and multiply. The sediment builds and builds. Left to ourselves the water gets cloudy, gritty, brackish. We become judgmental, more cynical, filled with the muck of despair.

What we need again and again is the transforming river of God's grace and forgiveness, the river that cleans out the sediment of our lives, the river that transforms the spirit and renews the soul.

Some of you may remember that over six years ago I preached from this same text. It was the text I used in what was a kind of trial sermon when I was a candidate for the role of pastor here at Salford. So why return to this text again? For the past six years it has been my privilege to be with many of you in hospitals from Allentown to Philadelphia to New York. I have had the privilege of sitting with you in your living rooms, at your dining tables, or in my office. At those and other times I have learned a little of your sorrows, tears, disappointments, hurts, discouragements. This is who we are—a people with flaws, failures, pain experienced and pain inflicted.

All of this takes its toll. And the spirit tends to weaken, the enthusiasm wanes, the vision is lowered. The residue and sediment from daily living weighs on us.

So I wanted to return to this wonderful, wonderful vision. Can we feel and experience anew the river of grace, the refreshing current of forgiveness, the ever-widening flow of God's love? The river is deep—so deep that it carries us. Where God is at work, there is no hopeless situation, no one beyond redemption, nothing from the past that needs to condemn us to a future given over to despair. Meanwhile, as we are renewed by grace and love, meanwhile along the bank, the trees grow, bear fruit, and generate leaves for healing.

I marvel and rejoice that every day in this community, through your work and ministry the sick are cared for, the troubled are given counsel, food is prepared and transported, buildings are repaired, young minds are taught, drugs and medicines are made available, and much more. Along the banks of the river there is refreshment, there is renewal, lives are changed and made fruitful.

Along the banks the community is transformed. There is life where the river flows.

Chapter 12

Vegetables with Love or Beef with Strife

SERIES: ASTOUNDING BIBLICAL VISIONS, PROMISES, EXPECTATIONS
May 17, 1998
Psalm 37:16-26; Proverbs 15:16-17; 16:8; 17:1

Vegetables and beef: "Better is a dinner of vegetables where love is, than a fatted ox and hatred with it." Why is a biblical writer concerned about such matters?

Perhaps this writer of Proverbs was ahead of the times. Did the writer know back then that too much cholesterol is not good? Or was the writer centuries ahead of the times in being concerned about efficiency in the food chain? Beef is not the most efficient use of resources. Many more persons can be fed if grain goes directly into food as compared to feeding grain to cattle and then eating beef. Perhaps the writer had an early read on the problem of world hunger.

While these are issues of current concern and conversation, I doubt that good or bad cholesterol or protein in the diet were on this writer's mind. The text is about dinner, particularly dinner with love. And we get the picture immediately. What is under review here is wholeness, contentment, the well-being of the family.

This is about as current a topic as you can get on to. And well it should be. A few years ago through a mistake in Houston, Texas, a child was summoned to jury duty. Someone observed that it was an inspired mistake. The children are the final jury before which a civilization should be judged.

How well are we doing in America society? What is the emotional health of the children in the schools? Are most of them entering kindergarten today generally in good health—mentally, spiritually, physically?

How are we doing here at Salford? I don't observe any malnutrition. The children here look energetic, inquisitive, able to quiet themselves during our "Focus on the Children." It is a joy to see them here. The children look wonderful.

And how are you as parents? Not perfect, of course. I know of no perfect families. Actually "pretty good" is good enough for children.

Parenting is incredibly complex and multi-dimensional. It calls for delicate balancing. What is the right combination of leniency and strictness? How does one hold the right amount of expectations and encouragement without expecting too much? In what measure should a parent be involved with a child's life, yet give the child space and freedom?

We could think of all kinds of related issues. But let's return to the text and think about dinner with love. Notice first that the writer uses the word *better*. Better is this than that. And that is the way it is. Choices need to be made all the time between the good and the best. That is what makes choosing so difficult and so critical. If choices in our families were simply between good and bad, good and evil, we could get on with things quickly and easily. What takes courage is turning aside from the good so that the best is found.

Of course, the text is dealing with more here than the menu. This is not really a debate over vegetables or beef. The issue is over vegetables with love, or beef with hatred. Under consideration here are issues of commitment, priorities, lifestyle, choices of where time and energy focus. What is interesting is an option the writer does not include. We would like the possibility of beef with love, better yet beef and gravy with love. But the writer does not offer that combination. Why not?

This is about more than meals. The writer is aiming at life, at choices. Beef signifies a life that is upscaling, that requires increasing amounts of energy, more work, more production, more time, more competence. Walter Brueggemann writes that beef with strife "refers to a busy family in which everyone is hustling to the limit. They arrive home for dinner too tired to care much, too exhausted to communicate, too preoccupied to invest in each other. Frayed nerves lead to worry, which leads to tension, and finally tears."[30] In a similar vein, Proverbs 17:1 states: "Better a dry morsel with quiet than a house full of feasting with strife."

What we are really after is a dinner with love. That's the goal. Our society thinks that love comes with the beef, or that beef is how the love is expressed, as if the house with the most toys has the most love. No. The writer wants dinner with love. That decision has priority.

A dinner with love is very possible. What does it look like? I'm an optimist here. A dinner with love is now just as possible as in earlier times, if not more so. We must focus on the better, and choose the best over the good.

Let me suggest three dimensions of vegetables with love. You could add more. But let's think about love as time, love as a direction, and love as no.

What are the things you remember in your years of childhood? What stands out? Is it not the celebrations, the times you were together and did things together? Perhaps it was a trip taken, a museum visited, a Phillies game attended, or the Sunday evenings spent leisurely around the table.

What children need is time—time to be with parents; time together as a family; time to converse about the events of the day, about the disappointments, the accomplishments, the fears, the joys. Mary Pipher in *The Shelter of Each Other* writes that "most of what children need, money cannot buy. Children need time and space, attention, affection, guidance and conversation."[31]

The TV and the computer are wonderful inventions, but they tend to work against time to be with, time to converse, time to laugh, time to share, time for bedtime stories, time to play together. Add it up some week—how many hours are spent in front of the TV or on the computer?

Even in busy schedules, ways can be found to be together. Work can be done together. I've found it more effective in getting children to work if I say, "Let's do this," rather than "You do that." Cooking and washing dishes can be done together. Even cleaning the garage together can be fun.

Families need rituals and traditions. These need not be expensive vacations. Some families set aside one evening a week as a kind of family time. The children help decide what to do.

Some families have yearly traditions—a day at the shore, taking in each year the Apple Butter Frolic, visiting an art museum or the aquarium in Camden or Baltimore. In our church library there is the book by Phyllis and Merle Good, *Ideas for Families*, which can offer some suggestions.

The point is, parents, that children will keep asking for more toys. But what they really want and need is more you.

Second, children need direction. We provide vegetables with love when we provide a direction. Children need to know what you are *for*. What is it you believe? What is at the center of your convictions as parents? What gives definition to your lives and to your life choices?

When parents are uncertain themselves about who they are and what they value, images from the broader culture will have a stronger influence. Mary Pipher puts it that "some parents have the impression that they shouldn't impose their values on their children. But if parents don't teach their children values, the culture will. Calvin Klein and R. J. Reynolds teach values."[32]

Children need to know what you think and why. They will decide sooner or later whether they will agree with your perspectives, but at least offer them a perspective. Not everything out there is of equal value. Not every opinion from the TV talk shows deserves consideration.

One writer suggests that good parents are a counter-culture: They counter the culture with deeper, richer values. The writer of Proverbs uses the word *better*.

If the space into which a child is born is a vacuum, how is the child to get oriented? If the impression is left that every belief, every conviction is of equal value, how in the world are children to find their way? For a generation or two now we have been so concerned not to impose on the next generation that we have left children vulnerable to the prevailing winds of the culture—and there are prevailing winds.

Third is love as No. Thomas Long, at one point a professor of homiletics at Princeton Seminary, tells the story of a student who asked to talk with him about her struggle. "I can preach love and I can preach hope and grace," she told Long, "but I cannot bring myself to preach about sin and judgment. There are already too many bad messages out there in people's lives, and I don't want to add one more burden."

Long reports that they pondered matters together for a time, then the subject changed to her teenage son, a drug abuser who was terrorizing the family with troubled and overbearing behavior. After noting that her husband's response was depression, Long's student, crying, told him that the night before, "I finally broke down. My son blew into the house and after hurling angry words at his dad and me, slammed the door to his room. I decided that enough was enough, and I went back there."

She admitted being intimidated by her large young son but proceeded anyway to confront him: "I love you so much I will not allow you to do this to yourself or to us anymore." Long observes that "We sat there for a moment, her words of the night before still hanging in the air. 'I think I have just heard,' I finally said, 'a powerful and faithful gospel sermon on sin and judgment.'"[33]

Vegetables with love does require that from time to time we say no. It need not be often. Someone suggests that the right proportion is about twenty positive comments for every negative one. But there must be limits. Some things are neither right nor necessary. Let the prohibitions be few, but let them be firm. No one said that your children need to think you are wonderful parents all the time.

The prevailing mood of the society in which we are parenting is that the way to good family life is more beef. The price of that is high—too high. The better way is vegetables. The highest value is not beef, but love.

A Father Latour put it that "when there is great love there are always miracles."[34] That is what we are after. And that is what is possible.

Chapter 13

Family Feuds
and God's Providence

SERIES: OLD TESTAMENT PERSONALITIES SEEK TO UNDERSTAND
GOD AS PROMISE MAKER AND COVENANT PARTNER

September 27, 1998
Genesis 37:1-11; 45:1-15

Would you have wanted your daughter to marry Joseph? Now that deserves a little consideration. By every appearance there is a lot to commend Joseph. You cannot help but notice him.

Early and late he showed imagination. Early and late he demonstrated responsibility. He was clearly a cut, quite a cut, above average. His SAT scores must have been quite high. He surely did well on aptitude tests.

He just may have been quite handsome. Potiphar's wife seemed to find him so.

So from about every angle that you might look at Joseph, he is rather interesting, quite capable. He holds considerable promise. You'll want to do it carefully, but you just might wish to encourage your daughter.

But before you start lining up a place for the reception, you might wish to give thought to one additional thing. It is often overlooked: When you marry, you not only marry the individual, you marry a family. That realization often hits later.

And Joseph had a family. Did he ever have a family! It was a houseful. The numbers of sisters we are not told for sure—we know of one. There were twelve sons—a whole baseball team, plus three on the bench.

One should not classify this family as dysfunctional. Let's rather say that there were family dynamics here. That there would be is understandable, since while all the children had the same father, they had four different mothers.

And Jacob, the father, did not help the situation. Among the children he had his favorites, special ones. Jacob, you may recall, was the favored son of his mother, and that had precipitated significant tension in his family. Now Jacob was perpetuating similar dynamics.

One can have a little sympathy for Jacob. The daughter of Laban whom Jacob really wanted was Rachel. Laban had given him the hand of Leah instead. But Jacob still wanted Rachel. The writer had noticed that Leah had lovely eyes, but of Rachel it is said that she was graceful and beautiful. Whether or not Jacob tried to treat his wives equally, despite himself, he favored Rachel more.

Then Rachel at first could not have children—"barren" is how the writers then always described this phenomenon. Finally, Rachel was with child; a boy was born. One can understand why this son named Joseph received a bit more attention. To add to the emotions, Rachel had a second son, Benjamin. In giving birth to him, she died. So one can understand Jacob's special care for Joseph and Benjamin. Would not his grief over Rachel transfer into special care for her sons?

Those of you with only one child avoid the problems of siblings. Is it really possible to treat each child equally, fairly, even-handedly? Some years ago I was conversing with several friends on the subject. The question was whether it is best for parents to try to treat each child with strict financial equality. If one goes to college, and you pay the college bill, should the one not going to college get the cash equivalent? Sometime this winter when you run out of things to discuss, we can spend an evening rolling that one around.

It often happens that parents seem to get along just swell with several of the children—but then have difficulty with one. Jacob's favoritism did seem a little too obvious. Joseph's brothers were assigned the tough tasks of caring for the animals day and night. Joseph got to run errands, probably stopping at the

Vernfield store from time to time for Double Stuff Oreo cookies for himself and Benjamin.

And Joseph certainly did not help himself in terms of his brothers. If he wanted to sit around and read poetry, at least he did not need to be quoting it to his brothers. And if he had those dreams, he could have described them to his sisters rather than taking up the brothers' time.

It is amazing what triggers resentments, conflicts, feelings in families. It does not take much. Let the idea emerge that one is getting a better deal. Or the brother or sister who gets a little more education is readily accused of getting a swelled head. When one gets a job promotion, new dynamics emerge.

So the feud between the brothers almost turned quite nasty—it did turn out more than moderately nasty. Credit Reuben and Judah for having a bit of heart.

I wonder what they did with the twenty pieces of silver the brothers got for selling Joseph into slavery? Possibly a lot of Double Stuff Oreo cookies.

The story goes on from there. Joseph initially lucked out in the slave market in Egypt. Potiphar noticed Joseph's soft hands and fair complexion and figured he probably had good experience around the house.

But Joseph's good fortune ended abruptly, and he landed in prison. After doing some time there, his propensity to pay attention to dreams paid off handily.

Now this is a cracking good story. The descendants of Joseph, generation after generation, loved it. It takes up nearly one-third of the book of Genesis. Will Joseph get out of the pit? Will he get out of prison? Will his brothers recognize him? Even though we know the outcome, at every turn we are still drawn into the intrigue.

But we have other things to consider here beyond the details of the story. Where is God in these events? What does Joseph know, and when does he know it? Does he sense some hand of God as these events unfold? How does he understand these dramatic turns of events?

The first thing we need to notice is that God is not very conspicuous in this story. Unlike in the stories of Abraham and Sarah or of Jacob, God does not appear dramatically. There are no reports that God came and spoke to Joseph. There are dreams here, but not dreams of a passageway that leads from heaven to earth. There is no wrestling with an unknown one through the night.

While there are references to God, there are no testimonies by Joseph that God spoke to him. In these stories Joseph and God are not in regular conversation. To discern the ways of God, Joseph had to keep his ear closer to the ground than did those who preceded him.

In Joseph's life story God is more hidden—not absent, but more in the background. The events of the story, the human activities, have the foreground.

Does this suggest that at times God is much involved in human affairs and at other times more distant? Does God attend intermittently to humans? Does God engage, then disengage?

Or might these stories rather indicate this: Even in the times of God's apparent absence, in the times of God's hiddenness, in the times when there is no stated word from the Lord, even then God just may be wonderfully at work.

That is precisely how Joseph understood it. He told his brothers, "God sent me before you to preserve for you a remnant on earth, and to keep alive for you many survivors." In chapter 50, the concluding chapter of Genesis, Joseph puts this thought in the form of a doxology: "Even though you intended to do harm to me, God intended it for good. . . ."

And here one anticipates the wonderful expression of Paul in Romans 8: "We know that in everything God works for good with those who love him, who are called according to his purpose."

The hands of God are not tied, not frustrated, not limited by sad and stupid things we have done and do. God's purposes are not fully thwarted by the sins of humankind, by the thoughtlessness and selfishness of men and women, by the shortsightedness of humanity.

Surely each of you, in ways small or large, has done something that was less than good, that was wrong, yet that somehow almost mysteriously, certainly unpredictably, led to something good. Such is the marvelous providence of God who somehow reconfigures the wreckage wrought by human activity into that which is good. What we do not know at any given time is the way the hidden hand of God is at work unnoticed.

Does that mean that it does not matter what we do? Is God's sovereignty such that God will bring good out of whatever wreckage we accomplish, and we live happily? Hardly.

The Joseph story has within it real tears, real tragedy, real suffering. There was cost. For years the brothers lived with guilt. For years Jacob mourned.

The point to remember is that while it may appear at any given time that God has taken a leave of absence, it just may be that God is wonderfully engaged. God is working for good even amid and despite human sin, family feuds, self-interest, and human selfishness.

One additional perspective on God shines like a beacon in these stories of Joseph. It is simply this—that while God cares for the children of Jacob, God also cares for the Egyptians. Yes, the children of Israel were fed, but the Egyptians also were fed.

Finally, back to Joseph. The book of Genesis contains a good measure of the human propensity for hatred and violence. It comes early in Cain and Abel. Hatred and revenge drives the story of Jacob and Esau.

Hatred is also central to the story of Joseph and his brothers. The text states bluntly that the brothers hated Joseph.

But Joseph breaks the chain. He does not retaliate. When his brothers come to Egypt, when the perfect opportunity presents itself to even the score and the score is uneven, when Joseph has the made-to-order opportunity to pay it all back, he does not. He chooses the road of reconciliation.

What would the world be like if at every turn we sought to disrupt the cycle of retaliation? What if, when another spoke ill of us, we chose not to speak ill of him or her? What if the unkind remark of the sister or brother was not returned, as it often is, ratcheted up a notch or two for good measure?

What if in the family feuds there were Josephs?

Chapter 14

An Astonishing Thing

LENTEN SERIES: WHEN IT HURTS TO LIVE—
CHRISTIAN FAITH IN DIFFICULT TIMES
March 14, 1999
John 9:1-41

What an intriguing text! Themes and sub-themes ebb and flow through the story. Scene 1 of the drama opens with a blind man. In the last scene those who see wonder whether or not they do. Jesus claims they do not yet.

In the middle scene, there is a repeated play on *who knows what*. In verses 20 and 30 the words "I know," "we know," and "do not know" occur at least ten times in all kinds of claims and counter-claims.

During a Christmas vacation in my sophomore year at Eastern Mennonite College, I was part of a gospel team that traveled from Virginia to Vermont, presenting programs in Mennonite congregations. There were five of us in the team—three men and two women—a mixed quartet plus one.

I don't fully recall what this extra person did in the program. He definitely could not sing, and I had grave questions as to whether he could preach.

What I do recall is that he was the principal driver of the Rambler station wagon. He always drove with a great sense of certainty that he knew where he was going.

His confidence was misplaced. We had written directions to all the congregations we were to visit to present programs, but if our friend had read them, he must have done so hastily. Time and again the rest of us in the automobile knew we were terribly lost before that possibility ever occurred to our friend the driver.

This story from John 9 ends on a rather dark note. Those who thought they could see actually could not see. But they did not know that they could not see.

Yet amid the somber tones, amid the story are wonderful little side comments, jabs in the ribs of the Pharisees, bits of sarcasm, much irony. We cannot help but smile. I'll try to keep this a bit on the light side today, so we can perhaps see ourselves in several of these scenes in the drama and be able to smile at ourselves a little.

The drama begins with a blind man—"blind from birth," it was reported. "Who is to blame?" the disciples wondered. One might have hoped that compassion would have been their first response, but when no one on the other side of the tracks is known personally, it is easier to see those living there as a class of people. My, my, they must have thought to themselves, how do people get themselves in the fixes they get themselves into?

So they ask Jesus who was responsible for this unfortunate situation. How do you explain this, Jesus? Why do bad things happen? Where does evil come from? Good questions, they thought. Wrong questions, said Jesus.

Blindness and darkness are not something for curiosity. They are occasions for redress. Do something, Jesus implied. We must work while there is time, when the opportunity affords itself. As Lesslie Newbegin has commented, the church of Christ is commissioned "not to explain the world, but to change it."[35]

Jesus makes a little mud pack and instructs the blind man to go and wash. He goes. Faith requires action, response—"Get up and walk." Unlike what happened in the story of Naaman the leper and Elisha in the Old Testament, where Naaman protested having to bathe in the muddy Jordan River, the blind man tapped his way through the streets, oblivious to the stares of onlookers wondering about the man with mud on his eyes.

Determined to give this a try, the blind man gets to the pool to wash. He sees! Can you imagine—bluebirds, roses, the faces of parents, nieces and nephews. And color. What amazing color!

Now you would have thought there would have been a celebration, a party—the biggest Apple Butter Frolic ever. But there was no party, only more discussion, more gossip. "Hey, remember the blind guy? They say he sees." "No, got to be someone else." "Doesn't quite look like him." "It is him. Did you ever notice that scar about his left eye—it *is* him."

"It is me," the no-longer blind man said. Still no party, but there was just a bit of a "Wow!" "Who did it?" "How did it happen?" He replied, "A man called Jesus, a little mud, go, wash. I went, and I see."

Clearly something new had hit town. It had to be the topic of conversation of the coffee crowds from the Energy Station to Mc-Donald's. Something was going on here. The order of things had shifted. Something, someone had a new angle, a different touch, a new strength, new possibilities.

Perhaps this had better be reviewed with those who know the order of things. So it is off to the Pharisees.

The story is told again with one more detail. It had been the Sabbath when the mud routine took place. That colored the opinion of some—wrong day they said; cannot be good, they concluded. "But the man sees," others countered. "Can good come from evil?"

"What do you think?" they asked the formerly blind man.

"He is a prophet," the man said.

Go get the parents. "Yes, he is our son," the parents acknowledged. "Yes, he was blind. More than that, we cannot say or choose not to say. Ask him, he is an adult."

Why is there such reluctance to acknowledge something new, something wonderful? Why do people want the world to stay as it is? Why do we want to stay the way we are?

The stakes get higher. The story is told again, now for at least the third time. "Give glory to God," the Pharisees say, or "Put your right hand on the Bible and swear to tell the truth, the whole truth, and nothing but the truth." But the focus of their concern is less on this wonderful change from blindness to sight, less on how it happened, less on what new possibilities were now available for the formerly blind man, as he moved from beggar to productive citizen. The focus is on how or who did it.

The blind man who now sees cannot keep himself from taking a little swipe at the Pharisees, teasing them, "Do you want to become his disciples?"

No, the system finds it hard to flex. The whole mindset cannot entertain the possibility that something new, wonderful, changed has arrived. The thought patterns cannot permit what theologian Edward Schillebeeckx calls the "divine positivity."[36]

So the you-know-we-know discussion ensues in earnest. We have heard it begin with the parents saying, "Yes, we know he is our son, we know he was blind, but beyond that we do not know."

The Pharisees also reiterate their baseline, what they know. "We know," they say, "that whoever did this is a sinner." We know, they imply, how things work, what is possible and what is not. They even drag out Moses, "We know that God has spoken to Moses. . . . "

But the stridency with which the "We know" comes out belies the shaky ground of their certainty. Reinhold Niebuhr wrote: "Frantic orthodoxy is never rooted in faith but in doubt." He added: "It is when we are not sure that we are doubly sure."[37] My friend, the driver for the gospel team, was convinced he was near the church we were looking for when in fact he was hopelessly lost.

The "We know, we surely know" insistence of the Pharisees elicits this wonderful response from the formerly blind man: "One thing I do know, that though I was blind, now I see."

And lest the religious leaders miss the point, he preached a pretty good sermon, pressing his message rather effectively. "It is an astonishing thing," he remarked in the opening lines of his sermon, "that something wonderfully wonderful has happened, and you do not know, or acknowledge, the source of it." And lest they forget their fundamental theology, he adds, "God is not beholden to sinners, but responds to those who worship and obey."

Underlying his discourse is of course the question, how can good come from evil? Something new, wonderful, truly good has happened, someone has brought new possibilities, the world has shifted, do you not get it? They did not get it.

Jesus meets the man again and asks the question at the heart of the gospel of John, the question the evangelist wants everyone to answer, we the readers included: "Do you believe?"

Here is the point on which everything turns. Do we believe or do we not believe that newness is possible, change an option? Do we or do we not believe that tomorrow need not be like yesterday? Do we or do we not believe that what got us into trouble last week need not get us into trouble this week? Do we or do we not believe that that which strains our relationships with family and friends now can be changed by the power and presence of Jesus?

Is the world doomed to continue on its course of injustice, violence, brokenness, everywhere and every time? Or can there be restoration, forgiveness, reconciliation? Are individuals left to find meaning and joy in life in their own strength alone? Is the universe and history simply a mindless configuration? Or can we believe that amid the seemingly random and chaotic there is a mind, and more importantly, a heart?

Shall we see the world only as it is with no insight as to how it can be? Have we convinced ourselves that the way we are is all that is possible? Shall we conclude that the blind beggars by the road deserve their position? Does anybody see?

Those who cannot permit the possibility of change, newness, restoration, reconciliation in themselves or in others will only see what they see. Those who choose to spend their time trying to figure out who is to blame will never get around to the wonderful and joyful work of healing and restoration. Those who think they see may not fully see.

The drama ends with just a little crack in the facade, the certainty, the double sureness of the Pharisees. One can imagine just a ray of light. Some of them asked Jesus, "Surely we are not blind, are we?"

Surely *we* are not blind, are we?

Chapter 15

The Second
Stage of Grace

SERIES: THE HOLY SPIRIT
April 25, 1999
2 Corinthians 3:12-18; 2 Peter 3:14-18

The younger of my two sisters married a Canadian. She has lived in Canada for more than thirty years. When she married this Canadian, she had about the same kind of Pennsylvania Dutch accent as I have—a little less, maybe. The amazing thing about my sister now is that she sounds like a Canadian.

Paul wrote to the church at Corinth, "And all of us, . . . seeing the glory of the Lord . . . are being transformed into the same image from one degree of glory to another; for this comes from the Lord, the Spirit" (2 Cor. 3:18).

The movement of the Christian life is from one accent to another. Remember the little courtyard scene when Jesus was being questioned by Caiaphas, the High Priest, the night before his crucifixion and Peter was in the courtyard? Peter was denying that he was associated with Jesus. Those nearby pressed the point, saying to Peter, "Your accent betrays you."

Eventually, our accent should be a dead giveaway. The whole demeanor of our lives should clearly indicate to which kingdom we belong.

Now changing an accent does not happen overnight. You have watched and heard young actors doing a play by an English writer trying to do a British accent—you smile at their effort.

The transformation of our lives, the changing of our accent, is a life-long project, never fully completed, never perfected here. But this acquiring of a different accent, this accent of Jesus, is what I call today the second stage of grace. Let me refer briefly to the first stage of grace, then talk about the second stage in two dimensions.

The classical definition of grace is "God's unmerited favor." Grace is receiving from God that which we did not deserve. It is receiving what we need, but could not attain. Grace is gift.

We emphasize that our salvation is by grace alone. Salvation is not passing some kind of achievement test. It is not meeting some kind of moral code. All our goodness does not cut it with God.

We cannot buy friendship with God. We cannot work our way into the kingdom by good deeds. We cannot marry our way into the kingdom. We cannot finesse our way to God.

God did not need to be nice to us. God simply chose to be nice. We deserved to be blamed, but God chose to forgive. We deserved to be abandoned by God, but instead God befriended us. That is grace—undeserved, surprising, amazing.

But to have received this grace, to be befriended, to be forgiven, to be redeemed, to use biblical language, is not the end of the road. To learn a new language, to genuinely take on a different accent, takes much more than practicing for a month. It does not happen quickly. We may well say that we have been converted, that we have changed direction, that we have turned from evil toward doing what is good—but the actual transformation of all the nooks and crannies of our lives takes time, a lot of time.

This transformation, this growing in grace, as Peter put it in the Scripture passage read, is the work of the Holy Spirit. In the study of church doctrine it is called *sanctification*.

The teachers in the Christian church spoke of the threefold work of the Trinity in this way—God as Creator, Jesus as Redeemer, the Spirit as Sanctifier. One person wrote that the fact that there is Father, Son, and Holy Spirit suggests that God knows and understands that we need more help than simply to be created and set going.

Remember that in the sending of space ships into space a number of rockets were needed. You had the first-stage rockets that sent the space ship out through the earth's atmosphere, but then additional rockets were needed to get the ship into orbit. Remember, too, that to be fully inoculated against a variety of diseases you get one little injection of a vaccine, then you need a booster shot.

These spiritual booster shots are the work of the Holy Spirit. The Spirit boosts the work of grace with an ongoing presence of energy, vitality, corrective influence that sends us on our way to being transformed from "one degree of glory" to another.

A very successful book was published some years ago with the title *Seven Habits of Highly Successful People*. There have been two sequels, I understand—*Seven Habits of Highly Successful Families* and *Seven Habits of Highly Successful Teenagers*. Diane Kropf suggested that perhaps this last book, *Seven Habits of Highly Successful Teenagers*, would provide good material for youth Sunday school discussion this summer. I looked at the book, and it surely has some good ideas. My little pause is the phrase *highly successful*—who ever said anyone is to be highly successful, and who defines highly successful? I would prefer highly happy.

But what I'm more interested in is the word *habits*. The title of another book some years ago was *Habits of the Heart*. Habits of the heart—that is an imaginative way of thinking about growing in grace.

Let us consider two ways whereby the Holy Spirit at work in our lives transforms us toward the image of Jesus. One way to be transformed is to welcome the scrutiny of the Spirit into our lives. What places in our lives are a little touchy? What things would we rather not admit are there? What shadows do we try to cover, not even acknowledging these to ourselves? Where are the secrets? Could we invite the Spirit to scrutinize our lives, touching the sore spots, softening those parts of our lives where we have been harsh, judgmental, critical?

Recently a training group working to combat racism was here to lead a training session for our child care workers, elders, church council, and pastoral team. We learned that we are more racist than we thought, and that we need the soft yet firm touch of God's Spirit to turn us to understanding and respect of others.

To walk more fully in God's ways we sometimes need a bit of an interruption, a jar, a word of counsel or admonition. A sign on a dirt road in Alaska had it, "Choose your rut well. You will be in it for the next twenty-five miles." Which ruts have we been in long enough? Have we been living in only the first stage of grace? Is it now time to move deeper into this second stage? Is it time to move to another degree of glory, as the Lord's Spirit confronts us and convicts us?

We know the general disposition of those being transformed from one degree of glory to another. Paul in Galatians lists the fruit of the Spirit. It is a wonderful list. "The fruit of the Spirit is love, joy, peace, patience, kindness, generosity, faithfulness, gentleness, and self-control." Now those are wonderful goals. A person with such qualities is one we would like to be with. A person like that is one we would like to be. The Spirit can move us along toward that kind of grace-filled life.

This leads to the second dimension of this second stage of grace. If one dimension is corrective, the second is constructive. Peter put it that we are to grow in grace. This is to learn a new language, to practice a new accent, to build.

This is not idleness. This is not simply wishing. We are not passive players here. This is not cruise control.

Rather, this is to catch a vision of a godly life and to discipline oneself to live it. The last two descriptions of the fruit of the Spirit mentioned above are faithfulness and self-control.

It is true that grace is God's unmerited favor, a free gift, undeserved love. However, the second stage of grace is an answering love. It is joyful response; it is being formed in the image of the one who is the clear expression of God's love.

An expression gaining attention these days is that of "spiritual formation." While those precise words are not used in Scripture to my knowledge, the idea is prominent in the New Testament epistles.

At times the forms of faith become too defined, too rigid. Then the form itself can squelch the Spirit, and for new experiences of faith to take hold, the old forms must give way.

I doubt, however, that a too-defined or too-rigid form is our danger at the moment. We have had several decades in church and society of breaking down the old forms—probably a needed direction. But the opposite danger may be our dilemma now. Ellen Charry wrote:

The view that emancipation alone enables human flourishing is flawed. An extremely permissive society, created
largely by the modern stress on emancipation is now spiritually harmful, just as a repressive society formerly was.[38]

To grow in grace is to be formed in our inner being. It is to be
centered. It is to know who we are and what we are about. It is to
have a rather clear idea of what kind of person we want to become. It is to give some kind of definition as to what our niche is
in the kingdom of God.

In their vision and intent, neither the Old Testament law nor
New Testament teachings are designed to be restrictive to
human well-being. Paul put it this way in the text read from 2
Corinthians 3: "Now the Lord is the Spirit, and where the Spirit
of the Lord is, there is freedom."

The biblical witness and expectation do not restrict the
human spirit; they give it focus and direction. "Love the Lord
your God with all your heart, all your mind, and all your
strength, and your neighbor as yourself" is expansive, not restrictive. As Ellen Charry put it, "God is committed to human
flourishing."[39]

Let us continue to welcome the ongoing work of the Spirit—
both corrective and constructive—in our lives.

Chapter 16

From One
of the Little Clans

FOURTH SUNDAY OF ADVENT
December 24, 2000
Micah 5:2-5a

Has this Advent season seemed long to you? The four Sundays seem like about seven or eight. Thanksgiving seems like a long time ago. We wanted to sing "Silent Night" and "Joy to the World," but it seemed we just kept singing "O Come, O Come, Immanuel." It's a little like having tomato soup for dinner night after night, while we know the Christmas ham is in the freezer.

Further, the biblical texts we consider during Advent are not the most upbeat or joyful. Every year the Advent texts we begin with are Scriptures that speak of the second coming of Christ. From them we are to learn to wait and watch. And then every year in Advent, sometimes for two Sundays, we need to hear that booming voice of that downer in the wilderness—John the Baptist. His message is about as far as it gets from "Silver Bells."

We want to get to the manger quickly. But pregnancies take nine months. The journey of the Wise Men from the East is long and difficult.

It is this long, long season of Advent that provides the occasion to consider anew that God's ways are God's ways—different, new, surprising. It is in the day after day of Advent that there is time to ponder, notice, reflect on the ways of God.

And it is during the days of Advent that we are invited, almost compelled, to wait and to consider our own setting, situation, dispositions. We are invited to ask ourselves what might limit the full measure of the Christ in us. What secret places of our lives have no room for Christ? Where does the crooked need to be straightened and the rough leveled so the King of Glory can come in?

Ah, but finally Bethlehem is in view. Mary is fully present and center stage. We do well to take a good amount of time considering the details of this event of the birth of the One who will bear the title of Lord and Savior. The details are significant.

These details are also of course familiar. But today we'll pause anew with two of them—Bethlehem and Mary.

The familiar hymn speaks of "O Little Town of Bethlehem." We might say "O Little Village of Bethlehem," for that is what it was.

A further detail comes from the text we have read in Micah. A family clan is mentioned—the little clan of Ephrathah. Scripture mentions this clan on two previous occasions. The mother-in-law of Ruth, Naomi by name, along with her husband Elimelech, were Ephrathites from Bethlehem. David, the shepherd boy who became the revered king of Israel, is referred to in the book of 1 Samuel as the son of an Ephrathite.

So there is double significance here: Jesus was born in a *little* village, and the lineage of Joseph, the husband-to-be of Mary, was from a *little* clan.

Similarly, mention should be made of Mary. Of her lineage we know less, which was not uncommon in the culture of the time. She was likely poor, now pregnant, and unmarried. The story's combination of details regarding this couple has to be significant—a village, a small clan, a woman poor, unmarried, pregnant. It is in such a setting that the momentous events unfold.

Now of course we students of Scripture know that this was not the first time God stepped into the events of earthly time in unexpected locations with unexpected people. God seemed to have a tendency to employ the unlikely for special purposes.

Sarah was barren. Gideon, youngest in the family, was from a small clan. David had to be called from the field. Now it was Joseph and Mary.

Of course God is not limited or confined exclusively to the poor. The prophets arose from all economic and cultural strata. But the point is clear: When God carries forward God's purposes, human estimates of status, power, influence, position, are completely irrelevant.

Mary, in contrast, did not miss the significance of the fact that she was favored for this very special and significant role, responsibility, and privilege. Her song is recorded in Luke 1:46-55, the themes of which we heard again this morning in the call to worship and the prayer of confession.

This memorable, beautiful, powerful song of Mary celebrated the deep and wonderful ways of God. From the margins God chose special partners who become powerful players in the sacred story. Persons so often overlooked, regarded as insignificant, were chosen by God for the lead roles in the wonderful drama. And Mary sings.

What does all this mean? Why are these details significant? Let me suggest some possibilities for what it means for us individually, what it means for the Christian church, and what it means in the world community.

The choice of the little clan and Mary means that no group, no family, no clan, no language, no race, no gender, no color is excluded from participation in the holy drama. Or to state it another way, anyone can be chosen for significant roles. No one here today is excluded from God's call and invitation to participate.

Since, then, God values all equally, so should we. We will regard each individual as of full worth. As we move amid the community, the check-out clerk at the grocery store gets the same respect and dignity as the store owner. The president of the company and the cleaning crew are paid equal deference. Those with clothes from K-Mart are valued as much as those with suits from Macy's.

The choice of a little clan and Mary also means that those who want to sing with Mary will be on the side of economic fairness and justice. Employers will pay a fair wage with benefits to all who work 40-45 hours a week. We will speak against public policies that hinder the poor from thriving. The growing gap between the very rich and the working class of this society surely is fully counter to the song of Mary.

Because it was the little clan and Mary who were chosen, we will never view the poor, the unfortunate, or those of lesser education as simple objects of our charity. Yes, we will be generous and gracious, but the recipients of our generosity will be our equals. We will listen to their wisdom. We will learn from them. We will value them.

Because of the song of Mary, no Mary dare be silenced, curbed, disregarded. Let the Christian church from Mennonite congregations to the Southern Baptist denomination halt their efforts to keep the Marys quiet, limited, to the side.

Today again we need to weep for so many places around the globe, where those from little clans suffer rather than sing because of violence, injustice, and suffering. Perhaps no place is more conspicuous today than Bethlehem itself, where tonight the songs of Mary will not be sung.

This year, when it was hoped that the music of Mary could swell in the streets of Bethlehem, they are empty, the shops are closed, the pilgrims are absent. The Christians sing in their homes. Intimidation and violence stalk the region. The Palestinians cannot travel freely; their olive groves have been cut down, their houses hit with bullets as the Israelis build new settlements in the land of the Palestinians. No song of Mary tonight in Bethlehem.

But Mary need not be silenced. Indeed she dare not be. What Mary needs is new voices. We are invited to pick up the tune, to add voices to the choir— each and all us, of whatever circumstance, of whatever name or clan. A medieval saint put it that we are all meant to be mothers of God.

Let the song of Mary emanate anew from our lives and from our lips. May Mary, through countless voices including our own, sing on and on and on.

Chapter 17

Overcoming Evil

THE SUNDAY AFTER 9-11
September 16, 2001
Psalm 45:1-11; Romans 12:14-21

In the memorial service for Dan Alderfer following Dan's tragic death by electrocution, I quoted the words of novelist William Faulkner. Those words seem apropos now: "There are some things for which three words are three too many, and three thousand words that many words too less, and this is one of them."[40]

After days and days of continuous news coverage, after innumerable replays of a plane striking the second World Trade Center tower; after countless color photos of wreckage and carnage; after many, many stories of loss filled with raw pain—more words would certainly be too many. Yet not to speak seems neither to fill emptiness nor confront disbelief and confusion.

When life changes radically, when a world shifts, when things are no longer the same, hasty words are not always the most perceptive, quick responses not always the wisest. Immediate analysis is often faulty; quick solutions often no solution at all. So today my thoughts are of a more modest sort, simply suggestions put forward for thought.

We are a community of faith, a community that turns regularly to the Scriptures in calm times, and all the more when times turn tumultuous. So in a moment such as this we shall let the themes of the faith stir our thought and imagination.

When evil seems to have the upper hand, we do well to search for the good, and there is much good in evidence. We give thanks and take encouragement from numerous expressions we have heard of human thoughtfulness, care, concern. Happily these have been duly noted by the president and the press: the dedication of rescue workers; the readiness of doctors, nurses and counselors to assist; the tremendous outpouring of good will and generosity—story after story emerges. The people of New York City, often represented as independent, uncaring, given to dog-eat-dog attitudes, have displayed remarkable care for neighbor and stranger.

Have you noticed those last words on cell phones to spouses, loved ones—"I love you." "Take care of the kids." All of us this week have hugged our loved ones with a little more intensity, and longer than heretofore. One must be grateful for the deep wells of goodness, care, thoughtfulness in the human family.

We are further moved by and most grateful for the outpouring of concern from other nations and peoples. Even some of them who are not viewed as the best of friends have offered sympathy and condolences to the people of the United States.

Those who themselves have known violence and suffering have been particularly moving in their words of comfort. A friend forwarded to us an e-mail message that comes from Palestinian Christians near Bethlehem, who in recent months have experienced their homes bulldozed, land seized, and families displaced. They write,

> With deep sorrow and profound grief we write this message to offer our heartfelt condolences to the mothers, fathers, children, friends and families of the thousands of innocent people who have been the victims of the terrorist attacks yesterday morning on the USA. We would like to reach out to all of our American friends to assure them that we stand by them at this difficult and tragic time.[41]

Another such message comes from the Justice and Peace Committee of the Colombian Mennonite Church:

> Dear beloved sisters and brothers,
> "In this time of uncertainty and sadness due to the recent tragedy in the United States, we want you to know that we are accompanying you, extending our love and solidarity to our family in the North.

In a country where the fear, anguish, and pain of war are seemingly permanent, we understand your hurting. We share your grief, confusion, and incomprehension. We too abhor this war that takes us further from Jesus' principles of justice and peace.[42]

And this word from Evie and Wally Shellenberger, Mennonite Central Committee workers in Iran, sent on Thursday:

"We gather to have our time of worship, just the two of us . . . today God spoke to us through a song, "I bind my heart this tide."

We started to read the second verse ["I bind my soul this day to the neighbor far away, And the stranger near at hand, in this town, and in this land"] tears flooded our eyes, our voices choked up. The words were much easier to sing at home, and the impact of their meaning hit hard. What does it mean for us to bind our soul to neighbors and strangers far away and near? We couldn't continue reading at that time. Our doorbell rang and after wiping the tears we answered. One of our neighbors held a warm loaf of bread in his hands to give to us. This was just another gesture of the caring and concern we have experienced here over the past days. As we, here as Christians bind our souls to our Muslim neighbors, they also of the Muslim faith, bind their souls with us."[43]

So there is a deep well of good will, love, care in the human family. We are grateful for the evidence of that, and our faith and hope remain encouraged.

But evil is also in evidence, etched now in the mind. Our emotions moved from not comprehending, to disbelief, to anger. How does one respond to such deeds and evil? Is there a word from our faith? Are there even modest suggestions? I have just a few, and you have undoubtedly thought of others.

Let it be recognized that the deeds of this past Tuesday were wrong. Nations and governments will appropriately seek to find the perpetrators of this kind of evil acts and if possible bring them to justice. Neither this society nor the world community can thrive when such horrendous deeds are carried out. No one can justify such acts against others in the human family. Horrible wrong has been done.

But while those who plot and carry out such deeds of violence need to be brought to justice, let us not condone indiscriminate violence. Indiscriminate violence is what we deplore. It is the killing of the innocent that is so doubly wrong. One columnist spoke of the law of unintended consequences. For every action, there is an excellent chance of producing an opposite and totally disproportionate reaction. So let our voices be raised, our prayers offered, that out of frustration, anger, and the cry for retaliation countless innocent will not be hurt.

I understand that the wife of a man who worked in the restaurant on top of the World Trade Center spoke of his death on television Friday evening in an interview with Barbara Walters. The man's wife said that as she thought of her husband and all that he stood for, she knew that he would not want others to be killed because he was killed.

Evil has been writ large. So what can be done? The president vows, as the local paper put it yesterday, to "rid the world of evil." The old methods will again be employed. Is there a better way?

Let violence not be perpetuated. An eye for an eye is at best only a temporary policy, probably not wise even now. It does not diminish the acts of harm and hurt.

What does it mean even now to overcome evil with good?

We can call for knowledge and understanding. Why are we Americans hated so? What causes such anger? Why is it directed against our society—its economic centers and its military center? While we as Americans perceive ourselves as noble, good, well-intentioned, why is it that others see this society as otherwise?

We must ask where oppression and violence are happening and where our society and our government are involved. Where are we in the wrong? Where is it that others feel exploited, demeaned, pushed aside, unrecognized, without a voice? How does our economic and military power so oppress people that hatred broods and broods?

We have seen the consequences when anger and bitterness reach extremes. Of course our anger has not reached those levels.

But we do well to ponder anger. Where in our hearts have anger and bitterness taken root in whatever measure? The Scriptures warn against bitterness brewing within the human spirit.

These are times for countless gestures of peace, love, care. Are there ways to reach out to others? Is it not time to find ways to greet the stranger more warmly? When hatred seems on the rise, let there be an extra measure of kindness. When anger spills out, let there be softer voices.

It is time for creative thinking. Our security is not found in larger defense budgets or stronger missile shields. We have reached the end of that road. Being the nation with the highest defense budget, a nation second to none, does not yield security or peace. To make the enemy even more of an enemy will not yield peace.

Shall we inflict more violence which will create the seedbed for a new generation inflamed by even more hatred and thirst for vengeance, plotting yet more creative ways to bring it to our shores?

We may well be at a moment of truth. Things are now different than they were. Can we think in new ways?

The old weapons, even though ever more sophisticated, no longer seem to work. Can we fight evil in the standard way?

Let new ways be tried, small, simple. We must reach out to neighbor near and far. These are times for gestures small and large. These are times for soft words, gentle actions, loving care.

Our security is no longer found in standard defense. Ships, planes, bombs can only do so much. Imagination is needed.

What if in Afghanistan, instead of unloading bombs and grenades, we offered bread, gifts, goats, sheep?

The president vows to rid the world of evil. We can understand his hope and intent. But the methods seem outdated, unpromising, doomed to failure.

Centuries ago another attempt was undertaken to rid the world of evil. That attempt is symbolized in churches around the world, on steeples, doors, communion tables, altars. It is the cross.

Perhaps it is time for the Christians of the world, of which we too are a part, to bear witness in word and deed to the alternative way to deal with evil. Every effort must be undertaken to overcome evil with good.

Chapter 18

The Right Tools

SECOND SUNDAY AFTER 9-11
September 23, 2001
Ephesians 6:10-20

These are very restless times. Even while we have tried to return to the regular routines, it is amazing how frequently our minds return to the events of Tuesday a week ago.

No matter how much we try to tell ourselves that things have begun to settle down a bit, we must acknowledge the presence of fear in some measure. Fear does stalk the land. From Washington to Hollywood to the Sears Tower in Chicago, on every commercial plane that leaves the runway, fear is present.

Surely as a nation we are far less secure. Whereas for many generations in this country weapons of war have been used in someone else's country, the weapons of destruction on September 11 were used only a few hours away from Harleysville. All of us with relatives and friends in New York or Washington immediately thought of the well-being of loved ones and acquaintances.

Now the truth is that our insecurity is precisely what many peoples of the world live with daily. In more places than we know or can name, the potential for destructive violence against home and kindred is there night and day. Let our thoughts and prayers be renewed for all who live daily with what people in New York and Washington have experienced recently.

Since September 11, evil appears more real to us than before—a theme I wish to return to later. We continue to wonder how and why some are given to such horrendous deeds. Not only did the hatred and evil lodge in their thoughts; with meticulous planning over weeks, months, perhaps years the anger, hatred, evil did not abate. Did not simple human decency, thoughts about pain, sorrow in any way enter the minds and hearts of the perpetrators?

Deep theological issues and questions linger in the aftermath of the horrific events. Is evil stronger than good? Did the God of light and goodness take temporary leave? How is it that the God who promised to be with us did not restrain evil, did not protect innocent people? How does one hold together the themes of human freedom and God's providence?

Some are saying that God's intervention kept them from the World Trade Center buildings, when normally they would have been there. But then why were others there as usual? Is God selective? If so, on what basis?

A few religious spokespersons have taken up the theme of judgment. They have suggested that these events are God's judgment for our country's moral laxity. To presume to know the mind of God is always to enter treacherous territory.

Thus we stand today with more questions than answers. Like the prophet Isaiah, we need to hear the testimony that God's thoughts and our thoughts are likely not the same. Much remains in the realm of mystery.

So fear, confusion, uncertainty live in the land. On Thursday evening the president tried, as the president should, to bring a sense of calm to the nation and to call the nation to an effort to curb these terrible deeds. A president by virtue of oath of office has promised to protect the people of the land. So this president spoke with some eloquence, and certainly with a sense of resoluteness.

Of course, I would have wished for more caution, threats far more limited in scope, promises to seek to protect the citizens of this country without so much antagonism toward others. So we shall continue to pray for our leaders and for restraint, wisdom, patience.

In a time such as this we are vividly reminded that we do live in two kingdoms. We have more than one loyalty. Jesus and Caesar do not speak the same language.

So if you will permit for another Sunday, I want to bring to mind themes of the faith and words of Scripture that provide orientation in these times—ways to think and speak. I will draw primarily from the text read from Ephesians 6, with reference to a few other texts as well.

From this text let me offer more about the nature of evil than I did last week. Then I will again call attention to alternate ways in which the Christian is called to address evil.

From where we sit, it is a little difficult to understand Paul's perspective in verses 10-12. We cannot know for sure how Paul saw the forces of evil at work. What did he mean when he spoke of cosmic powers? Did he see the forces of evil located somewhere in the space between heaven and earth, as verse 12 taken literally would suggest?

Perhaps two comments which speak to our situation can be drawn from these verses. First, evil is real. In calmer times, the fact of evil is not very present in our minds. We are apt to think that perhaps some kind of collective chiropractic treatment or an enormous massage is about what is needed. If we could all tinker with our lives a bit, perhaps all would be well. On the national scene, if we could ratchet up the religious piety a notch or two, perhaps evil would flee.

Not so, says Paul. Evil is strong. To combat it, Paul insists we need to "be strong in the Lord, and in the strength of his power. Put on the whole armor of God."

A second and most significant point to be observed here is that evil is not lodged in a few evil people. If we thought that, it would follow that if we could hunt down the terrorists, topple a few notorious leaders, contain certain so-called rogue nations, all would be well, and evil would be curbed.

No, evil is far more pervasive than that. It is intermingled with the good, with that which is necessary. We enjoy and view the American way of life as desirable and largely good, but there are others for whom it feels exploitative. We see capitalism as the most desirable economic system, but it has its underside, as those on the lowest end know too well. Profits are seen as essential to a viable economic system, but profits at whose expense?

Human governments are certainly essential. A society cannot function without law, order, protection of the weak from the powerful, and much more. But governments function with tremendous self-interest, and who would suggest that any government is without flaw?

Even personally, we know all too well that evil still has its tentacles in our lives. We are not immune to evil thoughts, mixed motives, harsh words, wrong judgments, and wrong actions.

Evil is real, pervasive, intermingled with good, sand grinding in every machine.

So what can be done? Paul suggests that we not presume to take on evil by ourselves. Evil does not quickly yield to our bright ideas, our initiatives, our best plans. More is needed—the strength of God's power.

But we are called to participate in the struggle. We are called to take up the whole armor of God. And here the proper tools are called for.

At times I wish Paul could have found other language and imagery than military, but here the use of such imagery heightens both the seriousness of the struggle and the contrasting methods. Paul calls for both defensive and offensive approaches. From this list let me call attention to three.

Fasten on the Belt of Truth, Paul suggests. Let us be vigilant in our truth-telling. In times of national stress, there is tremendous temptation to misrepresent, overstate, tell only part of the story.

On Thursday night the president helpfully made clear that not all Islamic peoples are terrorists, and that these persons should be welcomed among us as neighbors. But truthfulness would also require that we hear the cries and anguish, the concerns and perspectives, of those we consider enemies. To call for justice would suggest that we hear all cries for justice. For there to be justice, it must be justice for all.

One of the seedbeds of extreme resentment in our world is the Middle East, where the decades-long tensions between Israel and the Palestinians continues to involve tremendous oppression and clear injustices. Watch the language. The Palestinians are frequently called "terrorists," and the Israeli response— often far more violent and pervasive—is characterized as "security efforts."

Words and images can be exceptionally powerful for good or ill. Let words, then, be measured and truthful.

Further, Paul writes, "As shoes for your feet, put on whatever will make you ready to proclaim the gospel of peace." If peace is the goal, then how one chooses to get there is important. Martin Luther King Jr. put it that, "The end is pre-existent in the means."[44] There is good reason to question whether true and lasting peace can come by violent means. In the short book of James, the writer states: "A harvest of righteousness is sown in peace for those who make peace."

To be sure, no two situations are the same; national and international issues are exceedingly complex. But one cannot help but remember that just a few decades ago every prediction was that in the situation of injustice, oppression, and racial tension in South Africa, change would come only by violent revolution. But emerging from prison came a Nelson Mandela with a different approach. Words proved more powerful and effective than swords.

Third, Paul calls for "the sword of the Spirit, which is the Word of God." Addressing ministers, William Willimon writes:

> One of our duties as pastors is to re-narrate people's lives in the light of the story of Jesus. This re-scripting shows us how our ordinary lives are caught up in the great drama of salvation. We have become victims of narratives inadequate for the truthful living of our lives—narratives derived from psychology, economics, sociology and other secular means of defining ourselves and what happens to us. But through teaching us a new way of seeing and naming, through new words, pastors can create new worlds for us.[45]

In these times, as those who follow Jesus we must think with Christ. In Philippians Paul had written, "Let this mind be in you which was also in Christ Jesus."

Almost every place you turn these days you see, "God Bless America." That is not totally wrong, except too limited. Our key text of Scripture is "For God so loved the *world*."

We are not cherished above other peoples. Our well-being is not more important than the well-being of others. Let our prayers ascend for us, but equally for others.

I love this land as you do. We all mourn the loss of fellow Americans. But we weep equally for those who die elsewhere of whatever language or nation. The mayor of New York spoke aright when he noted that many persons of nations of birth other than the United States died there twelve days ago. So let our embrace be wide, our compassion extended to stranger as well as friend.

Finally, in the text from Ephesians 6 Paul encourages prayer. But what does he mean by his instruction to "pray in the Spirit"?

Might it be that if our prayers are dictated only by our fears, our needs, and our wants, they are too narrow, perhaps only from our perspective, as we see and experience things? To pray in the Spirit may be to pray more from the mind of Christ.

Then there is an added personal request: "Pray also for me, so that when I speak, a message may be given to make known with boldness *the mystery of the gospel*."

That mystery deserves another sermon sometime. Earlier in Ephesians, in chapter 3 in particular, Paul had written of how this mystery had been made known to him. What he saw as the mystery was that the Gentiles "have become fellow heirs, members of the same body, and sharers in the promise in Christ through the gospel." We will return to this theme next week in sermons from the book of Galatians.

At its core, the gospel is a reconciling gospel. It joins people together. Strangers become friends. The poor are received. Enemies are brought together. The "how this is accomplished in Christ" is the mystery of the gospel, and it is wonderful indeed.

Chapter 19

Neither, Nor, Rather

SERIES: ONE IN CHRIST—THE MESSAGE OF GALATIANS
November 25, 2001
Galatians 6:11-18

John Howard Yoder was a Mennonite theologian and teacher who died several years ago. Clearly, he was the most influential theological thinker in the Mennonite church. His writings are now greatly respected by those who study theology and ethics across the Christian denominations in North America and beyond. Several years ago Yoder was listed as among the most influential of twentieth-century theologians.

Now John Yoder was not particularly gifted in chitchat. His ability to make easy conversation with the man on the street may have been a bit deficient. Some would have said his relational skills could have been developed a bit more. He never went far out of his way to make students feel exceptionally gifted. He could be quite intimidating.

Often, when you would respond to one of Yoder's lectures with a question, he would not respond to the question you asked but instead tell you that it was really the wrong question. He would then proceed to state the question that should have been asked.

There is something like this "You got the question wrong" going on in the book of Galatians. Apparently, some teachers had been infiltrating these emerging congregations in the region of Galatia, suggesting that the faith as it was currently being understood and practiced there was not adequate. These teachers suggested that if you really wanted to be a Bible-believing Christian, if you wanted to be a full gospel church, if you wanted to make sure you had true religion, you would incorporate into your religion the key expectations of the Old Testament law. Of course, you would continue to believe in Jesus, but to make sure you were on the right path to true faith, you would add these additional ceremonies and practices.

When Paul heard of this full gospel or full Bible-believing movement, he almost went bananas. He would have none of it. What was promoted as an additional insurance policy, Paul said, blatantly undercut the status of membership in the new community of faith. Calling for ceremonies, practices, legal expectations, Paul argued, in reality denied the understanding of the faith. Salvation was not to be earned; indeed it could not be earned. Salvation was a gift.

Paul reminded the people in the Galatian congregations that we become part of God's family not by our own smarts, not by achievement of academic degree, not by special proficiency in a variety of spiritual exercises, not by multiple faithful service awards. We are part of the family by adoption.

Neither biological family name nor lack of criminal record really cuts it with God. Indeed those with surnames quite unfamiliar and those whose criminal or behavioral record is rather long can stand with equal status in God's family. For the family is fully by God's initiative, and is *received*, received in faith.

The gospel story is that God wills a phenomenally large family gathered around a phenomenally large table with only one head. That head is Jesus, our crucified Savior, or, as the book of Revelation puts it, a lamb as though it had been slain.

Thus these teachers who had concocted some kind of merit system, some kind of "we are better than you" system, a superior class system, stirred Paul's anger to a rather high pitch. Even at the end of this letter, Paul gets in one last swipe at them. It appears that earlier in the letter, Paul may have dictated his thoughts to a secretary, but at the end he puts his own pen to the papyrus. Lest anyone miss the message, he writes big and bold, not with an extra fine pen, but with we might call Magic Markers, in black, underlined.

Once again, Paul is not particularly diplomatic. Here he questions not only the actual teaching of these teachers but also their motives. He implies that in their teaching they are trying to score points with the big shots somewhere else. Further, Paul accuses these teachers of preaching and teaching things so that they can defend themselves against possible persecution. And as if that were not enough, Paul accuses them of blatant inconsistency—calling for observance of the law while they themselves do not fully observe it.

As we have noted on previous Sundays, these texts from Galatians have served the church well whenever rules, regulations, defined expectations have become too rigid, too locked into practices that made sense at one time but no longer do. Further, these texts have resonated through the centuries of the Christian church whenever, which tends to be rather frequently, any understanding creeps in that our status with God is achieved by our goodness, our hard work, our human efforts. Here in Galatians, once and for all, Paul effectively destroys this script of salvation as merit-based. And so the great cry of freedom from rules, regulations, faith as obligation rises triumphant from Galatians.

But just about the time that there is dancing in the streets over this new liberation, this freedom from rules and regulations, Paul counters with, "No, that's not it either—wrong question." Freedom is surely exhilarating, but in and of itself it carries its own dangers and temptations, its own tendency to another imprisonment. To simply be out from under the law, liberating as that is, is not to forge a new direction. Indeed, Paul warned that those who cry "freedom, freedom" will very likely quickly become beholden to their own self-centered humanity. Or, as Jesus had suggested, if you get rid of one evil spirit, but do not fill your life with what is good, evil spirits will return in greater number. Meaningful freedom in life is more than the spring flings of college students on the beaches of Florida.

So Paul says that if circumcision is not the solution, neither is uncircumcision. If law is not where it is at, neither is anti-law, or absence of law. If rules and regulations are unhelpful, the lack of these is likewise unhelpful. With his letters printed big, bold, underlined, Paul summarizes, "For neither circumcision nor uncircumcision is anything, but a new creation is everything."

This is the first time Paul has used this image—a "new creation"—in Galatians. You recall that the same phrase is in the correspondence to the church at Corinth, in which Paul had written, "So if anyone is in Christ, there is a new creation—everything old has passed away; see, everything has become new" (2 Cor. 5:17). But whereas Paul had not used this phrase or image before in Galatians, he had begun to sketch this new creation's nature and character.

Let's recall these dimensions. This new creation means freedom from any convictions that we can or must make ourselves good enough to meet God's expectations. We are freed from any notion that we can dress ourselves up well enough to get to meet heavenly expectations. No high-class department store has the dress or the suit good enough for the heavenly party. It cannot be bought.

Our human efforts to reach perfection are doomed to failure and yield only a great sense of failure and guilt. Righteousness, the kind God desires, is a gift. We receive it.

But there is more. God's gift in Christ is not only forgiveness, grace, mercy. God's gift is also a gift of Spirit, gift of Presence, gift of vision, gift of direction.

When we are freed from the law, this hope to be good, to live right, comes by the presence of the Spirit by which we are empowered in the direction of good and right. We are given focus and direction, a vision—to love the neighbor. And just when we think, okay, here we go again, we *must* love the neighbor—lo the very Spirit given moves us in that direction, for the fruit of the Spirit is love.

Neither law nor absence of law, neither obligation nor lack of obligation, quite describe the new reality. There is transformation, change, reorientation. The old habits lose a bit of the grip. This is more than forgiveness from the mistakes of yesterday. The old patterns are changed.

In our homes, marriages, and relationships this is not the same old same old. No—destructive patterns are broken, newness comes, behavior is modified.

This is not again our gritting our teeth and saying ten times to ourselves, This time I will do it! By the very power and presence of Christ, this is dying to the old and rising to the new in that power and presence.

And life's direction changes. No longer are money, power, recognition in and of themselves the goal. If we are given such things, we use them simply to benefit others. They have no value in and of themselves.

We begin to see with new eyes. We see others with new glasses. No longer are there rich and poor, no longer are persons valued according to position, race, or gender. Instead each person is seen as a special child of God, and each is highly esteemed and recognized.

Lo and behold, when these folk on the road of new creation gather, live and serve and work together, the gathering begins to look like something long lost and about which we dream. Then we remember it is the memory of paradise and also the dream of the New Jerusalem. Oh, we are a terribly, terribly long way off, but the scent of it caught in the evening breeze is incredibly sweet.

Chapter 20

On Earth As in Heaven

SERIES: THE STYLE AND DEMEANOR OF THE CHRISTIAN
July 7, 2002
Matthew 6:5-15

Prayer is a rather popular theme these days. The little book by Bruce Wilkinson, *The Prayer of Jabez: Breaking Through to the Blessed Life*, has sold surprisingly well. You have seen reports on studies claiming that persons who pray, or are prayed for, recover from illnesses more quickly and more completely.

Surely prayer is to be encouraged. The Scriptures again and again encourage prayer. "Pray without ceasing" is a New Testament text. "Ask and it shall be given, knock and it shall be opened, seek and you will find," are words of Jesus. Another text suggests that "the prayer of a righteous person avails much."

In considering the life and practice of Jesus, we cannot miss how often the gospel writers recorded that Jesus withdrew to pray. Prayer preceded important occasions in the life of our Lord.

And, of course, we know that our Scriptures contain more than a few prayers of individuals: Solomon's prayer at the dedication of the temple, the prayer of Jesus for the disciples, and many more. Public prayers of God's people are included in the Psalms.

So prayer is surely a significant part of the Christian life. One might note parenthetically that our Muslim friends practice prayer with greater regularity and intentionality than Christians.

But one must be honest and admit that some questions surround the practice of prayer. If God knows what we need, as Jesus suggested in the text read, why is prayer necessary? And what is the effect of prayer? Do our prayers change God's mind? Do they cause God to act? If we do not pray, does God withhold what is good? Do one hundred people praying have more influence on God than ten?

And what if good people are praying for different things? One group of people pray that it will be a nice day because of an outdoor wedding; neighboring farmers pray for rain so the soybeans will grow.

I've noticed already two teams before a game pausing to pray. Are they praying for the other team to win? Do they pray that they might win? Does God really care?

I'm reminded of the story of a big football game between Texas and Nebraska, played on Nebraska's home field. A local pastor was asked to offer the opening prayer, which went a little like this: "Lord, bless Nebraska and Lord bless Texas. But bless Nebraska a tiny bit more."

We are invited to pray. We are invited in the Scriptures to ask. But not any old prayer will do. James wrote: "You do not receive because you ask wrongly," or in the King James Version it reads, "You do not have because you ask amiss." I like that word *amiss,* which conveys the idea of "off the mark."

In considering prayer, how to pray, and for what to pray, we do well to turn again and again to the prayer our Lord taught us. From this familiar prayer, let me offer a few thoughts.

Prayer is in and of itself a confession. It is an acknowledgment of One beyond us. It is a turning from our own self-centeredness, our own self-confidence, our own sense of independence, our own "I can do this on my own" attitude. It is the recognition of a power and presence beyond us.

Prayer is a confession that there is beyond us One who sees more than we, has a perspective larger than ours, is the source of wisdom greater than ours. It is an acknowledgment and acceptance that we are not God, that we are creatures and not the Creator. Prayer is an act of reverent humility.

What struck me particularly this week in reflecting again on this prayer was the phrase *on earth as it is in heaven.* What caught my attention is that that is ever possible, thinkable.

Whatever heaven is, it is surely a realm of good, blessing, peace, reconciliation, joy, and all the attributes we long for and envision. Our Lord taught us to pray, to invite, to anticipate that these joys can be known and experienced in some measure here, and we pray then for greater measure.

The phrase *Thy kingdom come* carries, of course, the same thought. Thus heaven and earth are not disconnected worlds, not without some possible measure of intermingling.

Perhaps we have given up too quickly at every level of our lives. Perhaps we have given up on ourselves, not expecting these qualities of grace to soak deeply into our lives. Perhaps we have given up on our relationships, marriages, families, not expecting that the wonderful gifts from above can penetrate our settings. Perhaps we have given up on the church, not really believing that, frail and flawed as it is, it can offer a whiff of the heavenly breezes. Perhaps we have given up on our world, assuming that there is nothing new under the sun.

But we are regularly encouraged to pray "Thy kingdom come, thy will be done, on earth as it is in heaven."

I wonder this: If we prayed this prayer more fervently, more regularly, with greater expectation, might we actually notice hopeful signs? Might we notice indicators of the kingdom breaking in, evidences of the music of heaven coming among us?

Years ago when as a family we would take a trip, the children always kept asking, "When will we get there?" We would suggest gently (and sometimes not so gently), that because of this single concern about getting there, so many interesting things along the way were being missed. We do well to honor and celebrate the occasions for seeing evidences all about us, on earth, of the beauty and joy of heaven in our midst.

The Lord's Prayer, almost without our notice, turns our prayers from self-focus to God-focus. The phrase *Thy will be done* transports us into another realm. It is true, is it not, that if we analyze our prayers, we find that they tend toward the "give me, bless me, protect me, do this, do that" kind of character?

Of course personal petition is in order and appropriate as part of any prayer. But the Lord's Prayer calls us to consider ways God might see things. Therein we are lifted beyond our self-centeredness. The Brazilian bishop Dom Helder Camara prayed, "Lord, may your grace help me to want what you want, to prefer what you prefer."[46] Therein lies the power and strength of the Lord 's Prayer—"Your kingdom come . . . Your will be done."

In this regard the prayer of Jabez comes up short: "Oh, that you would bless me indeed, and enlarge my territory, that your hand would be with me, and that you would keep me from evil" (1 Chron. 4:10). It is only the last phrase that rings true to the Lord 's Prayer.

Thus we might well reflect on the leanings of our prayers. We might want to check whether our wants are in conformity with God's desires for us and others. We might want to ask, If our prayers are answered according to our requests, what effect is there on others? Surely God wills good for all, not only us.

In our local paper in a weekly column that local pastors submit, a Lutheran pastor this week—Fourth of July week—reminded the readers of a wider prayer. It is a prayer from the *1946 Presbyterian Book of Common Worship* able to celebrate both the beauties of our own land, with "skies bluer than the ocean," but also "skies . . . everywhere as blue as mine." And so "This is my prayer, O Lord of all earth's kingdoms," the prayer concludes,

> thy kingdom come, on earth thy will be done;
> let Christ be lifted up till all shall serve him,
> and hearts united learn to live as one:
> O hear my prayer, thou God of all the nations.
> Myself I give thee—let thy will be done.

Imagine prayers for the well-being of all. Imagine a family, a community, a society, a world where God's will, God's ways, are breaking out all around, and earth is beginning to look a little like heaven. Pray for it. Wait, watch, notice. Pray. And give thanks.

Chapter 21

You Will See Him Back Home and At Work

EASTER
April 20, 2003
Mark 16:1-8

What a way to end a Gospel: "So they went out and fled from the tomb, for terror and amazement had seized them; and they said nothing to anyone, for they were afraid." But that is the way the gospel of Mark likely ended.

If you have one of the newer translations of the Bible—the New International Version, or the New Revised Standard Version, you will notice various notations after verse 8. The NRSV lists a possible short addition to the ending of Mark, then also includes a longer ending—listed as verses 9-20. The NIV ends the gospel with verse 8, then there is the note that the most reliable manuscripts of the New Testament do not have verses 9-20, but then the NIV includes those additional verses. It is now pretty well agreed by biblical scholars that the gospel of Mark did end with verse 8.

This year, in the cycle of suggested Scriptures for Easter Sunday, we are given the resurrection story from Mark's Gospel. So for this Easter Sunday we will stay with this Gospel's account and ponder what we are to see and learn from it.

Now a lot is said in this account, in these last eight verses. Among the key aspects of Mark's brief account in the eight verses of Chapter 16 we notice these:

- The women went to the tomb early with spices. (Chapter 15 had ended with the women seeing where the body had been laid.)
- On the way to the tomb, the women worried about the stone. They discussed who would remove it or how it would be removed.
- When they entered the tomb, they saw a young man dressed in white.
- The young man acknowledged they were at the right place to look for Jesus, who had been crucified, but the body was no longer there.
- The young man said, "He has been raised."
- The women were commissioned to go and give that news in Galilee. The young man said they would see Jesus there.

Then the text ends with the report, "So they went out and fled from the tomb, for terror and amazement had seized them; and they said nothing to anyone, for they were afraid."

At the outset of Mark's Gospel, the writer had put it that this was "The beginning of the good news of Jesus Christ, the Son of God." Now this abrupt ending: "said nothing to anyone. . . ." What a way to end a Gospel!

Here there are no post-resurrection appearances of Jesus, no story of Mary Magdalene in the garden. No Emmaus Road conversation. No appearances in an upper room with disciples. No breakfasts by the lakeshore. We ask, "How were they to know of his resurrection?"

But perhaps Mark's word, his depiction of the resurrection story, is appropriate for us. For where are we to meet the reality of the resurrected Jesus? We are not in the Garden, we are not on the Emmaus Road. The home with the upper room has likely fallen down and been built over several times. No one really knows with absolute certainty where Jesus' tomb was.

How and where are we to come to the realization of the risen Lord? This story has a number of suggestions: Let me note three, and there are more.

The first way the resurrection reality presses in on us is through pondering the stone.Many mornings we wonder how stones will be moved. We lie awake in the darkness of pre-dawn, wondering what the day or week or month may bring.

In our life journey many difficulties arise, many obstacles confront us, many things cause us considerable worry. Our lives gather a variety of uncertainties, and we wonder how they will be overcome. Who will roll the stone away?

Now to be sure, the stones we face are not as large as the stone before the tomb. Nevertheless, have there not been many times in your experience when what looked excessively hard was somehow surmounted—a stone had been rolled? Perhaps it was only in retrospect that you realized that indeed something had moved, that a hand, a power larger than our own had been present.

Second, we should consider the import of the message of the young man. Dressed in white, he was surely a messenger to the women, telling them that back in Galilee they would see the presence of the resurrected Jesus. Of course, Galilee was back home. Galilee was the eight-to-five routine. Galilee was where life was lived.

It is one thing to know spiritual energy in the gardens of our lives, the high moments of worship, mountaintop experiences, Jerusalem settings. But it is quite another thing to know power and presence, the more-than-the-ordinary, right amid the ordinary at home and at work. But the man in the tomb said, "You'll see him back there in Galilee."

The question, of course, is this: Where does one look? Ah, one looks at the times and places where Jesus had been when he was in Galilee. Where Jesus had been, the blind saw, the hungry were fed, those with confused minds got clarity, those whose bodies and souls were paralyzed gained strength. The children were blessed. The poor were noticed. The rich young ruler was told that Enron did not yield joy and meaning. The crowds learned that in sharing loaves and fish multiplication can happen, there can be food for all.

Back at Galilee the disciples came to realize that where they *had* seen him, they *would* see him. As the story of Jesus replayed in their hearts and minds, the disciples finally saw it that you can win by losing, that to be first may indeed be to come up short, that to win the enemy over, you do not destroy the enemy.

Third, we comprehend resurrection truth when we realize to whom it was in the story that the women were to tell the news. They were to tell the disciples and Peter.

When Richard Nixon won a second term as president, he wanted to have a new beginning, so he dismissed his entire cabinet. Jesus did not hire new employees. Yes, they had all failed him, all deserted, all come up miserably short. They could hardly have done worse. They slept, abandoned, denied. But the crew was not fired. No—"Tell the disciples, and Peter."

We may well have failed a variety of spiritual driver's tests. We surely have failed a whole variety of spiritual exams. We too have come up short, sometimes painfully so, and cumulatively. But with Jesus we are still on the team, still on the roster. We are called to give it another whirl—back in Galilee.

Tom Long tells the story of being at a North Carolina conference center when the mountains were clothed in fall glory and of signing up for a bus trip along the Blue Ridge Parkway. He found himself seated next to a man who "announced in conspiratorial tones, 'I used to be an evangelist, you know.'" Long admits this didn't quite fit his hopes for the afternoon,

> But I was trapped, and he went on. "Yes, I preached all through these hills—little towns, small churches, tent meetings. I preached hundreds of messages. But then, one day, I realized I had been preaching the wrong thing."
>
> Now I was intrigued. "Preaching the wrong thing?"
>
> "Yeah, the wrong thing. I thought that the gospel was a list of things people have to believe. You know, 'Folks, you have to believe this and you have to believe that or God's gonna send you to hell.' That sort of thing. But one day I was reading the Bible, trying to get up a sermon, and it hit me like a thunderstorm, that's not the gospel! The gospel doesn't say, "You gotta believe this and that." The gospel says, "Friends, I have some good news. Hey, we don't have to live this way any more!"[47]

Resurrection is more than empty tomb. It is more than a garden visit. It is about stones moved. It is about powers of evil defeated. It is about power to overcome the demons of every age including our own—demons of consumerism, nationalism, militarism, a sex-saturated culture, and more.

Resurrection reality is to be embraced anew, to be welcomed back, to be told you belong. Tell Peter. Tell everyone in Galilee. Tell them that demons controlling hearts and minds can be put to flight. Tell them that stones can be moved.

Chapter 22

No Pre-Washed Jeans

SERIES: JOYS AND CHALLENGES FACED
BY THE EARLY CHURCH IN THE BOOK OF ACTS
October 12, 2003
Acts 26:12-18; Philippians 3:7-11

Judging by the amount of advertising space given to blue jeans, there must be a good market for them. Now I take it that many customers do not prefer jeans that look spanking new. Stiff blue denim is not the thing. In a Bloomingdale's advertisement, I saw pictured a pair faded around the pockets. Another pair looked worn at the knees. A third pair actually had a little tear above the knee like it was nicked on a barbed-wire fence. I think I have seen jeans that were pre-frayed. Now if Bloomingdale's would like jeans with a variety of interesting stains, I could supply a few.

Blue jeans made with a well-worn look! New store-bought jeans which look like they have seen the wear-and-tear of life! Living the gospel is more than buying pre-washed jeans. Let's explore how.

In recent weeks we have been looking at the story of the Christian church in its earliest years as told in the book of Acts. The full title of the book of Acts is listed in our Bibles as "The Acts of the Apostles." However, on reading this book you quickly notice that there is another actor, another mover and initiator, namely, the Holy Spirit. So some have suggested that the longer title should be, "The Acts of the Holy Spirit."

What we have been paying attention to in the sermons thus far is the way in which the circle widens in the faith community. This community has its roots in the Jewish faith but has been changed and transformed by the life, teachings, death, and resurrection of Jesus, the Messiah. It is now under the direction of the Holy Spirit. Under the Spirit's direction, this community is now encompassing, embracing, and calling to faith persons beyond those of Jewish background.

The expanding circle began with the cousins, the Samaritans, then embraced a person who had been a kind of stepson of the faith—an Ethiopian. And would you believe, while it took a series of visions and dramatic incidents, Peter came to see that even Gentiles were welcomed by God into this enlarging community of faith? We can hardly overstate that breakthrough. It would be something like the Jewish people today having dinner with Palestinians.

Of course, new issues needed to be faced. Which traditions to retain and which to discard needed discussion and attention. What were the core values to embrace?

I'll address that issue in a few weeks. But for today, let's step back a bit from this overarching drama to consider the effects of these new experiences, these paradigm shifts, as such are called today, on persons in the story. What was changing in the hearts and minds of these people?

We will, of course, need to make some assumptions here, since none of the apostles or other early church leaders provided us with an autobiography. We do not have "My Story" written by Simon Peter, or Saint Paul writing "My Personal Journey from Tarsus to Rome."

What we have in the book of Acts is a whole variety of people turning, changing, being grasped by a new vision, encountering the living Christ in the person of the Holy Spirit. What we have in short are multiple stories of conversion. The persons converted are an interesting variety—a jailer, a soldier, an Ethiopian, a raging enemy, not to mention many unnamed persons.

So, it seems appropriate to step back and ponder how this observer of and writer about the early church community pictures what it means to enter this new community. How did people come? What happened? What were the consequences? How were their lives changed?

This is, of course, an important issue, for in church circles today there is much talk about "church growth." "Evangelism" was an earlier term; "winning souls" was even earlier language. What does conversion mean? What might be expected of those embracing the faith? Indeed, what should be expected of us who claim to have embraced the faith?

Are there observations we can glean from the book of Acts? Let me suggest several among many potential ones.

First, conversion is likely more a process than an instantaneous event. When was Peter converted? Was it when he was called to follow Jesus? Was it when he offered that great confession, "You are the Christ"? Was it when he "wept bitterly" after denying Jesus three times? Was it in the post-resurrection call of Jesus to "feed my lambs"? Was it at the house of Cornelius, when Peter realized God's embrace was larger than his?

Second, conversion is fundamentally reorientation. This is perhaps best dramatized by the story of Paul. It is significant that Paul's conversion story is told three times in Acts. At least one point cannot be missed in this retelling—it is substantive, fundamental, utterly life-changing.

I wish to pause at this point, because I'm not sure that this is how the gospel is often presented these days. One gets the impression that Christian faith is something added on. We are American Christians—with *American* stated first.

Miroslav Volf observes that "the faith that people embrace is . . . shaping their lives less and less. The faith seems not so much an integral way of life as an energizing and consoling aura added to the business of a life shaped by factors other than faith."[48]

It seems to me that much of the understanding today is that faith is an added value. It is a little like the cereal boxes that are a little taller than before, and carry the words "20% More." Faith becomes a kind of bonus—a kind of icing on the cake we have already baked ourselves.

The claim of God on our lives reorients, turns us around whether quickly or slowly, in major steps or series of small ones. It is about change. When one signs on to the community of faith, this is not a special enhancement of life—something added to a normal life. It is rather a reordering of all of one's life from the ground up.

A third meaning of conversion is that it is to be summoned, called up. Inherent in Paul's conversion event were not only forgiveness, turning from the ways of persecution, but a summons to serve. The word of Jesus to Paul on the Damascus Road was, "I am sending you."

Conversion is about vocation. It is about being called to something more than the accumulation of goods, more than frequent trips to the mall, more than the search for the interesting and exotic. It is the fundamental summons to love God and love the neighbor.

It may take time to figure out in what specific ways to do that. The direction itself, however, is clear. I suppose much of our Christian journey is trying to love God with heart, mind, soul, and trying to figure out and practice love for the neighbor.

Fourth, conversion is about covenant—entering it, living under its terms, and surprisingly, enjoying or delighting in it. We do not do well to suggest that to become and to be a Christian are easy. To suggest that one only needs to believe, or have faith, or simply accept—here is not the full story. The gospel is about a relationship, a covenant. This is a partnership. And, there are expectations. Walter Brueggemann wrote that "our most serious relationships, including our relationship to the God of the gospel, are, at the same time, *profoundly unconditional* and *massively conditional.*"[49]

Perhaps one way to understand this is in terms of the husband-wife relationship. In one sense, that relationship is unconditional. The wedding vows suggest that nothing in the ebb and flow of life should sever the relationship—neither sickness nor health, neither poverty nor riches. Marriage is not a fair weather commitment. On the other hand, the relationship only thrives with reciprocity; love and the tokens of love shared, attentiveness, and responsiveness are inherent.

Likewise, in the Christian relationship with God, attentiveness to the promise given is essential. Response is inherent in the relationship. There are all kinds of clues and expectations which cannot be disregarded if the relationship is to be meaningful and truthful.

It is interesting, is it not, that Paul, often interpreted to mean that salvation is by grace and faith alone, writes in Philippians: "I want to know Christ and the power of his resurrection and the sharing of his sufferings by becoming like him in death, if somehow I may attain the resurrection from the dead."

This is no notion of "only believe, just accept." This is not purchasing pre-washed jeans. It is living faithfully in the rough and tumble and excitement of life.

Barbara Brown Taylor writes that "we tend to speak of becoming a Christian as if it were the easiest thing in the world to do."[50] Believing and accepting are a beginning, important to be sure, but becoming a Christian is also a journey, one in which believing and accepting reoccur again and again in ever new and deeper and larger ways.

We may buy these pre-washed, pre-frayed jeans. But we know what they are. We are not fooled. Nothing genuine comes on the cheap. We know that that which is meaningful, satisfying—yes, joyful!—comes with discipline, work, effort. No one builds physical stamina in front of the TV.

The really cool jeans are those that have been truly washed again and again. These may well show a tear here and there, a stain or two, perhaps even a patch, edges frayed. These speak of God having been loved and neighbor served. When you see that evidence, you know life has been rich, worthwhile, filled with meaning.

Chapter 23

Down to Joppa

SERIES: THE STORIES OF RUTH, ESTHER, AND JONAH
February 15, 2004
Jonah 1

You have to sort of admire this guy Jonah. He has got guts. It was Martin Luther who said, likely tongue in cheek as he echoed and distorted the Apostle Paul, that if you are going to sin, sin boldly. Do it right, in other words. In the book of Revelation, the writer reports God's wish for one of the churches—the church at Laodicea—"I wish that you were either cold or hot. . . . " It is lukewarmness that gets under the skin.

Well, Jonah was anything but lukewarm. In the story, he is decisive, cuts it clean. God says go northeast; Jonah heads southwest. Go to Nineveh. Jonah goes to Joppa. Be a witness in Scranton. Jonah takes the first express bus to Atlantic City. And since Joppa is not far enough from Nineveh, Jonah hops the first boat out of Joppa—Tarshish sounds great! Now we have on our hands a drama. It looks like we have here a collision course.

This reminds me of the story I heard told by Bill Snyder, then Executive Secretary of Mennonite Central Committee. As I recall the story, it went something like this. A young man was being trained to serve as a switchman on the railroad to make sure trains would get on the right set of tracks. After days and weeks of training, the instructor sought to see if the lad was prepared to operate the controls. So he posed the question, "If you had one train coming from the east at forty miles an hour and another coming from the west at thirty miles an hour, with both trains on the same set of tracks, what would you do?" The lad replied that he would fetch his brother.

Surprised and dismayed, the instructor asked why he would do that. The lad replied, "Because my brother has never seen a train wreck."

The Jonah story starts out looking like a wreck in the making. God wants Jonah to head in one direction, and Jonah heads the other way. The principal actors in this drama are fully at odds. Today we will consider how Jonah saw things—then next Sunday, how God saw things.

Before we turn fully to Jonah, however, there are two or three places we ought to pause just briefly in the drama to note some interesting things along the way—places, as it were, where we ought to pull off the road to see a little of the scenery.

Did you notice that the sailors are respectfully portrayed? They are not believers in Jonah's God. How could they be? Jonah is in no mood to give any witness to anyone. He is down in the mouth and down in the boat. He is asleep.

But when the sailors hit the tempestuous sea, they called on whatever god or gods they had. When they were convinced that Jonah was the reason for the terrible storm, and Jonah said, "Put me over," the sailors tried desperately to not have to do this.

Finally, after very reluctantly throwing Jonah overboard, they prayed to Jonah's God and pleaded for mercy. Rather admirable fellows.

A second thing we might wish to notice is found in chapter 4. At two places animals are mentioned. In this story God's concern for the animals is noted. We are reminded that the Creator not only pays attention to humankind but also keeps an abiding concern for the other dimensions of the Creation—here, animals. It is a fitting reminder.

A third place to pause is with the situation of Jonah in the belly of the fish. I do not know who had the worse deal here— Jonah in the fish, or the fish having Jonah stirring around. Apparently, things were not too bad for Jonah. It seems he had a kind of three-day spiritual retreat. From the belly of the fish Jonah created a wonderful psalm. It is recorded in chapter 2.

But back to Jonah's call. Why did he not want to go to Nineveh? What might those first exposed to this story have heard in it?

The city of Nineveh was part of the Assyrian empire, indeed for a time served as the capital city of Assyria. It was located on the Tigris River in the region that is now Iraq. It had been Assyria that had conquered the northern kingdom of Israel. It was not a friendly takeover. So the Hebrew people had no love for the Assyrians. There was bad blood here, very bad blood. This is why Nineveh would have been about the last place a prophet like Jonah would have wanted to go to start a church. The thought of having Assyrians as brothers and sisters in the faith would not have struck the Hebrews as a swell idea.

But let's hang out with Jonah a little longer. Why did he not want to go?

Jonah is not the first person in the story of faith reluctant to go and preach. In fact, foot-dragging prophets make up a distinguished list. Moses protested God's call. He claimed he was not the best speaker. So God had to bring along Aaron. Jeremiah likewise protested that he could not speak well. He claimed he was inexperienced. "I am only a boy," he said. Elijah, you know, almost entirely lost his serve, or his confidence, about mid-career, and hunkered down. Both Amos and Isaiah shuddered to think of the message they were called to announce.

Today across nearly all denominations, too few persons are planning and training for pastoral leadership. Our own denomination is no exception. All across the church now efforts are underway to determine the causes of this upcoming leadership shortage and to seek to correct it. Various ideas are floating about as to why too few young and not so young persons are not sensing a call to ministry.

Perhaps each possibility has some merit. Some suggest that parents are not wishing for their children to consider ministry. Perhaps business, medicine, education, or engineering are set forth as more desirable vocations.

Some suggest that there are too many stories of pastoral leaders and congregations being unable to get along, so people shy away from ministry which carries the potential for conflict. Some say that expectations are broader than what a person can fulfill; the gifts expected are not carried in one person.

All the above and more may have some elements of truth. Next week I hope to comment on why I believe and have found ministry to be a wonderful privilege, but for today let me add my bit as to why there may be a pastoral shortage.

It is because the message we are called to carry and announce is a hard one to carry. To go to Nineveh is tough. So we go down to Joppa.

Let me tell you how preachers "go to Joppa." They shape the message so it sounds easier. Or more accurately, to "go to Joppa" is to emphasize part of the message, to keep emphasizing only a part, and to leave other parts aside.

It is the temptation to preach primarily on the "Prayer of Jabez," for example.

It is to tell stories of courage, success—this is called motivational preaching. It is to emphasize that people need support—called therapeutic preaching.

It is to preach about sin, but be selective about which sins. The preacher cannot go wrong, of course, in railing against drugs, pornography, sexual promiscuity, abortion as a means of birth control.

Of course, these and other sins need attention. But woe to the preacher who condemns the sins of greed, over-consumption, injustice, racism, arrogance, pride, lack of concern for the poor, insensitivity to the neighbor. I find it interesting that Jonah is placed in the Bible right next to Micah and just about next to Amos—two of the great prophets of social justice.

What makes preaching hard is that the message is so hard. "He that would save his life shall lose it." "He who would be first among you, let him be servant of all." "If your right eye causes you to sin, tear it out and throw it away. . . . " "And if your right hand causes you to sin, cut it off, and throw it away. . . . " "If your enemy hunger, feed him. . . . " Any volunteers? So we go down to Joppa.

Of course we would rather sing "Praise God from whom all blessings flow" than "Dear Lord and Father of mankind, forgive our foolish ways." Of course we prefer singing praise songs to yearning for the healing river whose waters will (as composer of "Oh Healing River" David Haas put it), "wash the blood from off the sand."

The roads to Joppa are many.

It gets even harder. When we read the texts we are called on to preach, not only do we well know that those to whom we preach may not like to hear this; we ourselves do not like to hear it.

In the story of our text, in the Word, we see our own sins. And we, like Isaiah, say, "Woe is me." Some days it is terribly tempting to go to Joppa. We preachers know Jonah.

And so do you. Oh, God's call to us may not be of Nineveh proportions, not so big a deal, not so clear-cut. Calls and choices come to us in smaller doses. T. S. Eliot used the image of life measured out in coffee spoons.

But how do we respond to God's call to us, God's nudgings, invitations, opportunities? And what might be our Joppa-like response? Perhaps we keep our lives full enough of this and that, activities for the sake of activities, to leave little time for Nineveh-type calls. Perhaps we permit the culture and climate of our time to define for us who deserves our time, who are the important people, and we'll leave the Nineveh types to themselves.

Next week we will notice that Jonah eventually went to Nineveh and eventually preached. But one gets the impression he did it with little enthusiasm or conviction.

It is possible to go to Nineveh—but really be in Joppa. There are ways to drag our feet, ways to say yes—but really say no. There are many ways to get to Joppa.

This Jonah is an interesting fellow. We know him. He is us. Again and again in our lives, in countless ways, small or large, in opportunities and options before us, likely every week in some measure and way, the issue is, "Nineveh or Joppa?"

Chapter 24

Baptism:
The Defining Event

July 18, 2004
2 Corinthians 5:11-20

A good part of our lives consists of efforts to improve our situations, to improve ourselves. This may be in relation to appearance—as when we may exercise to be more fit. Many try to lose weight. Some change a hair style or undergo cosmetic surgery. These are efforts at self-improvement.

Surely, the pursuit of education is for purposes of improvement—growth in wisdom and understanding. At times we change jobs to gain greater opportunity. Some choose entirely new vocations to pursue interests and abilities heretofore unexplored.

In our spiritual journeys we likewise seek movement and growth. We resolve to be more attentive to others, listen more carefully, care more deeply. We consider a variety of spiritual disciplines—meditation on Scripture, prayer, and other spiritual exercises. So, in many and varied dimensions of life we are on a pilgrimage of growth and development.

Our text read from 2 Corinthians interestingly speaks more dramatically and comprehensively than merely of growth or self-improvement. Paul wrote, "If anyone is in Christ, there is a new creation: everything old has passed away; see, everything has become new." This is more than a new hairstyle, a new job, revised habits. The language of the New Testament is bold, dramatic, all-encompassing. The imagery is that of conversion, change, reorientation.

Baptism is the public expression of that commitment of foundational orientation. Now to be sure this change from old to new looks more conspicuous when someone is dramatically converted, for example, from being a drug dealer to being a Christian. But the issue is not what we came from. The issue is the direction we choose to go.

The New Testament descriptions of the meaning of baptism employ a number of dramatic images. It is a crossing over from wilderness to Promised Land. It is moving from slavery to freedom. It is going under the water and rising again. It is dying and being resurrected. In today's text it is moving from old to new.

On this Baptism Sunday, from this text in 2 Corinthians, I wish to have us ponder some dimensions of this new creation. I will suggest four—all interrelated.

The first dimension is the realization that there is Another for us. We are not alone in this world. We are not unprotected from the powers and forces of evil. We are not battling human limitations and tendencies by ourselves. Christ, who loved deeply enough to accept death, urges us on.

This is not necessarily the idea that Christ died as our substitute. Rather it is the notion of solidarity, of *being with*. In the way in which Adam's sin casts a pall on all humanity, so in Christ's death and resurrection we are privileged to participate in Christ's victory over evil and death.

At the very center of history a transforming action has taken place. The powers of evil have received a mortal blow. And the one who dealt the mortal blow stands in solidarity with us. Sin and evil still exist—but need no longer be decisive. Truly to accept the new creation is to live in this realization.

A second dimension of this new creation is to enlist in a new community. It is to join a people. There is no escaping it—we are defined by the groups we join, and ultimately, we are defined by which group provides the primary definition.

From youth to our elderly years we are part of a whole host of groups—high school classes or college classes, professional organizations, volunteer organizations and much, much more.

Some weeks ago I was reflecting on this when I attended my forty-fifth high school class reunion. I graduated from Boyertown High School class of 1959. I'm intrigued by class reunions. At the fifth or tenth reunion, the colleges attended and degrees received seem important. By the fifteenth or twentieth, it is positions that seem important. By the twenty-fifth or thirtieth, it is the number of grandchildren that sparks commentary.

By the forty-fifth, a kind of social leveling has taken place. There have now been enough battles with cancer, say, or enough of life's disappointments to make position, status, and wealth fade into the background. No longer does it matter who were the bright and beautiful, the three-letter athletes, the heads of the classes.

At the forty-fifth reunion I felt a kind of human solidarity. But the high school class of 1959 makes up a small piece of who I am. My identity came to the fore again when along with some family members I checked out the new Phillies stadium—Citizen's Park. On the occasion of the singing of the national anthem I realized that I'm an American. But that is not my primary allegiance.

We could go on and on naming groupings of which we become a part. The issue is—which is defining, which is foundational, which orients our lives? It is in baptism that we publicly declare our signature community. The Christian journey is not a "my God and I" journey—it is a "God and God's people" journey. It is a people's journey for a number of reasons. I name two.

One is that we enter a stream that has been flowing for centuries. We are indeed the recipients of the faithful witness of forebears of the faith from Abraham and Sarah to grandparents and parents. The Christian journey is not "bowling alone" or bicycling alone. It is riding a train filled with saints of time past and present.

A second dimension of this people journey is that the witness of the faith is a communal one. It is the witness of an alternative community. The dimensions of faith only become visible as a new community is being formed.

Robert Frost, writing of two roads diverging and the less traveled one taken concludes, "And that has made all the difference." Which people we join, which community defines us, makes all the difference.

From Wilmington to Dover, Delaware, Route 13 and Route 1 run quite parallel. If you wish, you can get off Route 1, travel a while on Route 13, and return to Route 1. Again and again the one crosses the other. At times they run for miles in sight of each other.

While we are part of the Christian community, enlisted in the people of God, much of the time we run quite parallel with other groupings—school, business, sports teams, professional organizations. We remain very much part of society, intermingling with others.

But if you want to get to Lewes, Delaware, to the beach, you have to stay on Route 1. At Dover they part, and if you stay on Route 13, you'll end up somewhere, but not at the shore.

It is at baptism that we declare we are on Route 1. We may parallel other roads from time to time, but it is Route 1 that is our road because we want to get to heaven's shore.

A third dimension of this new creation is *to be called*. There are few things sadder than to sense persons nearing the end of life who still haven't figured out who they are, what their calling is.

Sisters and brothers, we have a calling. We are chosen. We are enlisted. We are ambassadors for Christ. Of course there are a thousand ways to live that out. But this calling is not only to church work. It is a calling to live with unique and peculiar dispositions. It is, in every vocation, during times of unemployment, underemployment, retirement, when still in school and after school, to declare and represent God's ways. It is to "Love the Lord our God with heart, soul, and mind, and the neighbor as oneself." I have not known anyone to run out of neighbors.

This calling is to take on the mind of Christ and the Spirit of Christ. It is to live no longer for ourselves but for and to serve others. Every worthwhile vocation, and every setting, and every week give multiple opportunities.

Fourth and finally, the goal and mission of our ambassadorship is not first and foremost to make people happy. It is a ministry of reconciliation. Ever since Adam and Eve were ushered, to put it kindly, out of the Garden, there has been layer upon layer of separation expressed as distrust, enmity, dislike, violence, and war. Separation: the signal mark of sin.

Our calling, our mission, is reconciliation. This task is not to return us to the Garden, some stage of innocence. It is to work at building the New Jerusalem.

And now I have circled back to community. This is a community enterprise; you only do it with others. Reconciliation is not something we see alone in the garden with God.

Our task and calling is to bring together that which is apart. The measure of the power of our witness is the degree to which the new community pulls off surprises—Jew and Gentile, would you believe, around the same table.

Now this is no easy task. Differences are real, experiences vary, opinions and perspectives are deeply held. In this world there are real divisions.

But here is the vision: to bring together that which few would predict possible. And even more surprising, it is to bring together not at the point of the lowest possible denominator; it is not simple compromise. It is more.

When a bone is broken, then knits and heals, we are told that where the healing has taken place, the bone is stronger than before it was broken. That is what we are after—to be stronger at the broken places.

These days many churches struggle over music and worship. So some solutions are worked out. Some have two services. Others say they have "blended" music. I'm not interested in blending. I want transcendent music!

This ministry of reconciliation is not easy for a whole variety of reasons. I mentioned a few differences of experience, different deeply held opinions. It is not easy because each of us is still on this pilgrimage of no longer living to ourselves. The old Adam and the old Eve have not yet been fully dunked and drowned in the river Jordan. Frederick Buechner has observed that "the old Adam and the old Eve are mighty good swimmers."[51] So we will have to work it out together. But when we permit God to pull us along in the ministry of reconciliation, the outcome is a wonder to behold. It is new creation!

Ronald, Sheldon, Liz, Isaac, John—today you give public witness to the direction you are headed. You choose to identify with a community that is your defining one. Your decision to be baptized, to be known as a Christian, means that other options have been turned aside from—other roads have been rejected.

On this journey you have chosen, know this. There is One who journeys with us, One in solidarity with us, One who, as the Scriptures suggest, sticks to us even closer than a brother.

Beyond that, on this journey you are accompanied by other pilgrims. The journey may on occasion seem lonely, but keep your eyes open, for the tennis courts are filled with other players, the stadium stands are filled with fans.

Finally, in baptism you sign on to a vision, a mission. It is to join hands with Jesus who through his continuing presence in the world, in the church, pursues this work of reconciliation, this creating of something new.

Chapter 25

All Invited

SERIES: DIFFICULT QUESTIONS IN THE FAITH
September 26, 2004
Matthew 15:21-28; Romans 10:14-21

On some subjects we can speak with far greater confidence and certainty than on others. For certain questions there are rather clear and often multiple biblical references.

On the issue or question of "How wide is God's mercy?" we are not as quickly on sure footing. Will persons of other faiths ultimately be received into God's eternal fellowship—or will they not? If they would be welcomed, on what basis would they be welcomed? Their good deeds? The sincerity with which they held their faith?

And if the door is opened to persons of other faiths even just a little, what are we to make of New Testament texts that speak of only one path to salvation? Last week I called attention to one of these texts from a sermon by Peter: "There is salvation in no one else, for there is no other name under heaven given among mortals by which we must be saved" (Acts 4:12).

There are those who suggest that this is the way it is. God has the freedom to draw things up as God might choose. If there is only one gate into the New Jerusalem, that is God's choice—who are we to question? Our task then is to try to see that as many as possible hear and learn this message of salvation by this path.

Others have been offended by this exclusivist view and have gone far to another side, suggesting that there are many paths to God, God has many names, and all who worship sincerely under whatever name are welcomed by this God of many names. With that premise, the task is to encourage persons of all religions to worship honorably, truthfully, sincerely.

Now of one thing we are certain. It is that God loves all people. God's love is so broad and deep that it is God's desire that all would be saved. God wills all to come. There is no question but that all are invited to enjoy the fellowship of God.

If then God wills all to come, if all are invited, and since God's love, mercy, and grace are so broad and deep, why has God apparently built only one door? Why did God not design the New Jerusalem with entrance places in every direction?

The Christian church's view that salvation is in Jesus has remained quite troublesome for many. Thus, some speculate that there might be other ways to enter the heavenly city. Some would suggest that if the quantity and quality of our deeds meet a certain measure, that will be the basis of entrance into the eternal city. There is little support for such an understanding in our Scripture, which holds that no one is sufficiently good to merit the heavenly prize.

Others have speculated that perhaps after death there will be a kind of second chance. These have offered the view that in some period after death and before some final accounting, people will clearly sense their need for God's mercy and in that setting God's grace will still be available. To that idea one must say that this is highly speculative. We do well to suggest that people should not bank on this second-chance idea.

So then, are we left with these opposing extremes that on the one hand the gate is a single gate, quite narrow, or on the other hand that there are multiple entrances and almost any path will do? Or might it be possible that God's mercy expressed in Christ is applicable to persons who do not have knowledge of this gift of God in Christ?

Let me illustrate this possibility in two concrete ways. First, it is our belief that children are covered by God's grace and mercy in their innocence, in their not-yet-awareness of the saving grace of Jesus. Here we believe God's grace and mercy in Jesus is available to these who have not yet come to comprehend this wonderful provision.

Second, it would certainly be our understanding that the saints of the Old Testament were to be graciously received by

God on the basis of their faith in a God who they believed had yet more to offer. They did not know the full dimension of God's saving initiatives, but surely they were commended for their faith in what God promised yet to do.

Let me try to illustrate in this way—and all illustrations are imperfect. Have you ever been invited to a party, an anniversary, a celebration of some kind, but for some reason the invitation never got to you—it was lost in the mail, the address was wrong, or whatever? Now that dilemma poses at least two questions. First, were you invited if you did not know you were invited? Would not the reasonable answer be that yes, you were invited even though you did not know you were invited? The second question is more important. Would you have gone had you known you were invited? Would you have responded had you received the invitation? That is the critical issue.

The two texts read from Matthew and from Romans push up windows a bit, letting in some interesting light on the status of those beyond the regular stream of faith.

The Matthew story deserves a sermon in its own right. Who was this Canaanite woman? Why does it appear that Jesus was uncharacteristically ungracious to her? But the incident ends with Jesus announcing the great faith of this woman and then honoring that faith.

The text from Romans 10 is located in the middle of an extended discussion by Paul concerning where Jews now stood in light of Jesus, since many had not accepted Jesus as God's Messiah. Were we to ponder this text in depth we would need to consider the settings and contexts of Paul's quoting from Isaiah, Deuteronomy, while assuming the understandings of those to whom he was writing. But what causes us to pause with this text is verse 20, "Then Isaiah is so bold as to say, 'I have been found by those who did not seek me; I have shown myself to those who did not ask for me.'"

From these and other texts we could cite, might it be that God's saving grace in Christ is already available, applicable to persons who have not yet heard or have not understood? Will God honor the faith of those who respond to the dimensions of God of which they are presently aware?

The biblical perspective is that there is some knowledge of God other than what is gained in the biblical story. Paul in the early chapters of Romans suggests that from creation itself there is knowledge of God. Paul wrote in Romans 1,

> For what can be known about God is plain to them, because God has shown it to them. Ever since the creation of the world his eternal power and divine nature, invisible though they are, have been understood and seen through the things he has made. (Rom. 1:19-20)

It is also our understanding that God is known in part in other religions. We cannot and dare not suggest that there is no good, no truth in other faiths. Can such faith, whatever its combination of truth and less than truth, be honored?

Might it be that God will count as righteousness this leaning toward the light, this honest search for truth, this eagerness to worship God as God is understood, if only partly? We believe God in God's abounding love and grace is seeking to redeem this world. Is that redemption restricted to only those who have heard? Or does it include those reaching for that which they do not yet understand?

So I'm back to my little illustration of the invitation to the party that did not arrive. Might God not honor the heart of those who surely would come to the celebration if they knew they were invited? Does God honor those with a clear disposition toward God as they currently understand God?

Now at least two questions remain. First, what about those who did receive the invitation but chose not to come? That I will address in a forthcoming sermon.

The second question: If God does recognize and honor the honest faith, the sincere worship of those who have not heard the message of Jesus, must we seek to take the message of Jesus to them? Should we let well enough alone?

I think not. It should give us great joy to give the message to those who are invited but are not yet fully aware of this. Is it not a wonderful privilege to share of what has been given to us to all those striving to live aright? Is it not a marvelous opportunity to report to all whose understanding is that God is quite demanding that in fact God has come to humankind, to us, in grace and love?

In the book of Acts there are these wonderful stories of persons of sincere searching faith who found with joy the story of

Jesus when told. You recall the story of Phillip and the Ethiopian who wondered of whom Isaiah was speaking. Or you recall the story of Peter and Cornelius who received with joy the message of Jesus.

Sharing our faith, whether with those not yet believers or persons of other religions, is not a one-way street. When we study another language, we gain new insight and understandings of our own language. So it is that when we converse with others on the themes of the faith, we too learn.

To the great eternal banquet, the banquet of banquets, all have been invited. Many have not yet received the invitation. Let us, let the church of Jesus Christ, continue to be diligent to deliver the invitation in word and deed.

Chapter 26

Suffering:
Why and for What?

SERIES: DIFFICULT QUESTIONS IN THE FAITH
October 17, 2004
Romans 8:18-27; Job 19:23-26

Intermittently this fall I've been speaking on what I have called difficult issues in the faith, or questions or issues for which we do not have complete or definitive answers.

If we wanted to, we could find quite a few questions to which the Bible or the experience of the church over the centuries do not provide quick and easy answers. And then new questions arise from time to time. Ethical and moral issues have arisen in our time over reproductive possibilities, genetic manipulation, matters related to prolongation of life, and much more.

While the Scriptures do not offer simple declarative statements on some issues, that does not suggest that they offer no perspectives. The very character of our Scriptures invites conversation, testing, reflection.

The Bible comes to us as story, poetry, parable, letter, and other literary and artistic forms. It comes to us in lived experience, not simply theoretical reflection—although one must say quickly, there is astute reflection in Scripture.

One of the pervasive human dilemmas and questions—it comes up so often—is the question of suffering. Why is there suffering? More perplexing, why is it experienced so unevenly? Why do the innocent suffer and some less than innocent seem to escape so much? Some pose the issue as a question of where God is when tragedy comes. Whether it is in the local or world news, such questions arise regularly. Experiences come when the spoken or unspoken word is "why?"

Now we know there are not final or complete answers to these questions. But this morning let's chip away at the issue.

Why is there suffering?

We can offer several reasons. First, there is physical suffering because we are human—created with bodies of limited duration. The body in time will weaken. Some or several of the bodily systems will succumb to disease or just cease to function. On that journey many, some more than others, experience pain, physical and emotional suffering.

Second, there is suffering because of wrong choices or decisions made over long periods of time, or wrong judgments that yield accidents. We drive too fast around a curve and slide off the side of the road. In haste, we trip and fall.

Third, there is much suffering because of human greed, ineffective and exploitative governments, human injustice, violence and war. Sin shows its ugly and tragic face at all levels of the human experience. A father abuses his wife and children. A teenager neglected by family members takes out the anger on peers at school. Ratchet this up, and a post-Holocaust Israeli seeking security takes a Palestinian's land, even as a Palestinian deprived of land hurls stones or a grenade at an Israeli.

The rich and powerful find ways militarily and economically to control resources and garner the wealth for themselves.

So injustice, starvation, violence is the global experience. The children die, the young seethe with anger, disease ravages the weak and vulnerable. Significant suffering is in the world as a result of human decisions or failure to decide aright.

But suffering results from things more difficult to explain. Four hurricanes strike Florida. The Haitians, among the poorest people of the world, suffer from floods.

There are additional questions. Why are some born with predispositions toward mental illness? Why are some born with physical limitations? Why do some children develop unusual diseases and die?

Why is it that some who take no thought for God, who live rather recklessly, nevertheless seem to prosper? This seeming unevenness or unfairness troubles the writers of the Psalms again and again.

So, the experiences of suffering come from many places—some from things we control, much arising from that which is beyond our choice or control.

When tragedy or suffering comes, there is this tendency to want to explain why. So those who have experienced the death of a child, the sudden death of a spouse, or other loss often try to answer the "why" question.

Some explanations are not helpful. One unhelpful explanation is that God must have some purpose, or that God is in control. This suggests that God is the source of tragedy—that God has some pre-established plan and everything follows a script.

Or sometimes one hears what are meant to be words of comfort to families experiencing loss: "God knows you are strong."

Or sometimes it is suggested that woe comes our way to discipline us—as though we deserve tragedy or suffering.

Tragedy and suffering come and indeed are distributed quite unevenly across the human family. For us the issue may not be so much to find a way to explain its occurrence, as to wrestle with how we respond, what we do amid such experiences, and what we learn from them.

Let me suggest possible outcomes from tragedy and suffering.

First, we tend to grow in understanding and empathy. There are those who having known pain and loss now live lives of deep compassion.

Second, experiences of suffering can have a disciplining effect. Priorities may be significantly adjusted. A sorting of the important and less important takes place.

Third, suffering, in ways we do not quite understand can train eyes and heart to see good and blessing and joy in new and remarkable ways.

Barbara Nkola from Zimbabwe spoke at our Franconia Mennonite Conference Center. Those of you who were at the World Conference in Bulawayo, Zimbabwe, would remember her as the one who, I believe, greeted the guests at each service.

Barbara Nkola is from a country where there is not enough food, a country living under a government making exceptionally poor choices, yet Barbara is a sister of joy. She reports that our sister churches in Zimbabwe are so very grateful that people came from all around the globe to sit with them, worship with them, experience their setting, know of their insecurity and suffering.

Suffering creates solidarity. Suffering creates community, deepens faith, sifts and sorts. And remarkably in suffering, a solid foundation is found.

Fourth, suffering can stimulate, elicit new and deeper insights. New and creative thinking does not necessarily come on the high tide of success.

It was during Israel's experience in Babylon that new and far deeper understandings of God and God's ways arose. In the history of the church insightful thoughts have come from writers while in prison. Paul wrote letters from prison. Some of the most insightful perspectives on the twentieth century are the *Letters and Papers from Prison* by Dietrich Bonhoeffer as well as the *Letters from a Birmingham Jail* by Martin Luther King Jr.

Fifth, suffering produces hope. That is the word of Paul in Romans 8. You would think that suffering might rather produce despair, and well it can. But suffering can turn one's eyes toward the future, in belief that the One who is Creator and Redeemer will bring the project to glorious completion.

Lewis Smedes wrote a memoir before his death called *My God and I*. In the book he wrote about the experience he and his wife had many years ago. It was the experience of his wife giving birth to a beautiful child who died before living fully one day. So Smedes ponders tragedy and suffering.

After 9-11, he pondered the question others have posed—"Where was God on September 11?" He wrote:

> For me, there was no mystery about where God was and what God was up to on the morning of September 11, 2001. God was right there doing what God always does in the presence of evil that is willed by humans—fighting it, resisting it, battling it, trying God's best to keep it from happening. This time evil won. God, we hope, will one day emerge triumphant over evil—though, on the way to that glad day, God sometimes takes a beating.[52]

Indeed it is in the periods of suffering, or perhaps when one moves in close to where there is suffering, that one experiences unusual depth of solidarity with others and unusual sense of God's presence.

I do not know what all Paul was suggesting in the text from Romans 8, but I find verse 26 arresting. "Likewise the Spirit helps us in our weakness; for we do not know how to pray as we ought, but that very Spirit intercedes with sighs too deep for words."

Is not Paul suggesting that in the very midst of suffering, amid our human groans, God in the Spirit is present, sighing or groaning as well? Did not Jesus say, "Lo, I am with you always?"

Finally, suffering brings humility. The complexity of the issue brings Job and his advisers ultimately to silence before the God who is greater. Suffering then has the remarkable possibility to produce faith, hope, and worship.

We do not seek suffering. But let us not fear it. For from it there is much to learn. Through suffering lives can be deepened, enriched, changed. And amid suffering we believe God touches down in very special ways.

Chapter 27

On the Journey
to Being Blessed

SERIES: THE SERMON ON THE MOUNT
January 2, 2005
Matthew 5:1-20

My youngest grandson and I often play the game "Sorry." I play the game with what I believe is the best strategy. I get as many of the four playing pieces out on the board as quickly as possible so each can move around the board toward "home."

My grandson employs a different strategy. He puts only one of the four pieces in play at a time. To my way of thinking that strategy limits the options he has. It does not make a lot of sense to me. To me it is, shall we say, counter-intuitive.

Now I have not kept an accurate count of who has won the greater number of the many games we have played. But my rough estimate is that my grandson's counter-intuitive strategy has resulted in his winning about seventy-percent of the games.

The Sermon on the Mount is, in many ways, counter-intuitive. It is so counter-intuitive that over the centuries interpreters have suggested alternative ways to understand these teachings other than taking them at face value.

Now nearly everyone agrees that the ideas and visions set forth here are wonderful—*ideal* is the word often used. Then, however, the "buts" are offered.

For example, some have suggested that perhaps individuals or individual relationships can rise to meet these expectations, but the ideas become impossible in communal or social behavior.

Others have posited that the early church assumed that the period of the church would be brief. Thus, perhaps one could achieve these ideals for a short period of time.

Then there are those who have suggested these ideas are so far out of reach that they remind us we are sinners. That is what drives us to appropriate repentance.

Over the next six Sundays, including today, we want to take another look at these teachings. I encourage you to read the sermon (Chapters 5-7) a number of times in weeks to come.

A few general observations are in order. As I noted in my sermon last Sunday, the writer of this Gospel makes many connections to the Older Testament. Here again a clear connection is made. You recall that the Ten Commandments were given to Moses on a mountain—Mt. Sinai. Here the sermon of Jesus, a key summary of the teachings of Jesus, is also given on a mountain.

The issues addressed in the sermon, we must admit, are crucial ones in life. Money, violence, anger, sex, anxiety, judging others, and more receive attention here.

A continuing theme in the sermon is the relationship of the teaching in this sermon, and the law (the teachings of the Older Testament). Is this simply the Ten Commandments Plus? Are the teachings here even more demanding than the earlier laws? Does Jesus go beyond the law, "adding to" as it were? Perhaps, but "adding to" does not quite describe what he is doing..

In the remainder of chapter 5, there are six, I believe, "antithetical" statements, as some call them. We have the repeated phrase, "You have heard that it was said. . . . But I say. . . . " Clearly, here Jesus is suggesting that not only are certain acts wrong, but the intent, the thought, is also wrong.

Now if it is not accurate to suggest that Jesus was simply adding to the law, what is the goal of his teaching? In verse 17 Jesus claims that his intent is certainly not to abolish the law, and he does not say his intent is simply to add to the law. Rather, he says he came to fulfill the law.

Might it be right to suggest that in the teachings of Jesus we find the key, the central, life-affirming, and life-giving dimensions of the law? Some suggest that Jesus got to the spirit of the law.

The story of Jesus in the Gospels reports on the occasions when Jesus actually violated the law, at least as it was commonly interpreted. He healed on the Sabbath day, for example. He had lunch with and associated with persons whose behavior clearly violated the law.

What we have in Jesus is a sifting and sorting of what were the central themes—sometimes referred to as the weightier dimensions—of the law. The themes of justice, mercy, love come to the fore. Concern for the neighbor had priority.

Now a word should be said about law. Actually, the more helpful word would be "teaching." There is this persistent notion that law inevitably is restrictive, that the expectations of the faith have the effect of limiting and squeezing the fun out of life, that the law makes the Christian journey a long list of do's and don'ts.

Perhaps it was true that as Hebrew faith developed over the centuries, and as it came to be practiced by some during the time of Jesus and Paul, layer upon layer of law had been added. Perhaps then the law felt like fences, barn doors, restrictions. But that was not the original intent.

The Torah was rather a way to life, to good order, to meaningful journey. Having been chosen by God for a special mission in the world, the Hebrews were given the guidance for living this special calling. Torah was to be the joyful roadway on the faith journey. Thus, the Psalmist could speak of the law as sweeter than honey.

It is to that vision that Jesus calls the disciples and the crowds in this sermon. In the text read from Matthew 5, the kingdom of heaven is mentioned three times and twice offered as present reality. The kingdom of heaven being at hand means that the joy, meaning, and fulfillment anticipated in the future era has already begun to take form and is to be experienced in this age.

The beauty, joy, richness of heart and soul anticipated in the future has already broken into this age where challenge, suffering, and more are still known and experienced. The Scriptures speak of foretaste. The taste and smell, the music and dance of the future has already begun to be experienced now.

The Christian community thus begins to live in the ways that demonstrate that vision. It is living now in the perspectives and ways that will characterize the age promised. Thus, Jesus said, "You are the light of the world. You are the salt of the earth."

Recently, I read of a man named Red Davis, who lived in Marshall, Texas. Twenty-five years ago he retired as the chief executive officer of a big company in east Texas.

Upon retirement he went to the pastor of his church to discuss how he might use his remaining years to serve the Lord. The pastor assumed that he might want to chair a major committee of the congregation. But Red said that he had heard that the Sunday school class of three- and four-year-olds needed a teacher. He said he would like that job.

For the next twenty-five years Red taught that children's class. On Saturday evenings he would call the children to ask about their week, and tell them he looked forward to seeing them on Sunday.

The children came.

It was said that at congregational business meetings that when Red Davis stood up to speak, a respectful listening happened—not because of his earlier career, but because children and parents knew of his love and dedication.

At his funeral service, the story was told of the woman in the local grocery store with her small child. The boy spoke to his mother saying, "Mom, I just saw God." The woman looked around. Sure enough, the child was pointing to Red Davis. The writer of this story commented, "When the little boy tried to wrap his mind around the very big idea of God, the best he could do was think of Red."[53]

You are the salt of the earth. You are the light of the world.

And Jesus did not picture this calling as burdensome. Rather he used the word *blessed*, a word quite difficult to translate. Translators have tried a variety of ways. "Good for you" is one effort. "Happy" is another.

On Thursday I caught a brief interview on National Public Radio with a psychologist who had written a book on living fully, meaningfully. The word she used was *exuberance*. Perhaps that gets at the promise of Jesus. It is to live in fullness, meaningfully, joyfully, exuberantly.

We do well to listen to this sermon by Jesus.

Chapter 28

The Donkey

PALM SUNDAY
March 20, 2005
Matthew 21:1-11; Philippians 2:5-8

Did you ever see pictures or drawings where little things in the picture were deliberately placed askew? These pictures were offered as a kind of challenge—see if you can find the nine things wrong in this picture. So, for example, you might find a boy in the picture with a baseball glove and one of the fingers would be missing. Or perhaps you would see an automobile in the picture with the door handle at the wrong place. Or you might note that in a house in the picture the curtain was upside-down.

This Palm Sunday parade at first glance looks like everything is properly in place. There is pomp and circumstance, as there should be in parades. The location is right—Jerusalem, the capital, the Holy City. The direction of the parade is, as it should be, toward the center of town.

Historians suggest that the Romans had pretty well perfected this kind of triumphal processions. A new ruler would march into a newly conquered city with appropriate accompaniment of troops, bands, a crowd corralled to line the streets. To the center of the city the new ruler would go.

All seems in place here for this parade. The crowds are there; celebration is in the air. The music fits the occasion. It's "Amazing Grace" and "God Bless America" themes rolled together— "Hosanna to the Son of David," "Hosanna in the highest heaven." People get in the mood, waving branches, lining the streets with whatever is handy.

Perhaps about midway along the parade route it occurs to some in the city that something in the picture isn't quite right. The curtain in the window is upside-down. There is something odd here, something askew. The music is right, the spontaneity engaging, the celebration spring-like. There is a kind of swelling of enthusiasm. It's like the quarterback in the football game eliciting the cheers of the crowd. The feeling grows that perhaps this is the year for the hometown team.

But something is out of character—a finger in the glove is missing. It is the donkey.

Make no mistake about it, this event was planned. Three of the gospel writers let it be known that this event had very careful thought behind it. The writer of this Gospel lets the reader "in the know" about this very careful planning. "Go into the village ahead of you, and immediately you will find a donkey tied, and a colt with her; untie them and bring them to me. If anyone says anything to you, just say this, 'The Lord needs them,' and he will send them immediately."

So it happened. The disciples went, and as luck would have it, lo and behold, just off Second Street by the side of a shed there was a donkey and a colt. Had the owner by chance just stepped into Abe's Mini-Mart for a cigar?

Who are we kidding? This was planned. The whole scene is "acted parable." This is street theater.

Bible readers know about this. When the people of Israel and other neighboring nations acted as though Babylon was an idle threat, Jeremiah the prophet tried to preach otherwise. The people did not listen.

So Jeremiah fashioned a yoke, put it around his neck, and ponderously walked up and down the streets of Jerusalem, saying, This is how it will be with you—you will be in captivity, you will be in bondage.

Ezekiel the prophet was even better at theater. He dug a hole in the side of the house. Then every morning he would emerge lugging packed suitcases to illustrate that a journey would be upcoming.

The prophet Hosea outdid them all. To demonstrate Israel's unfaithfulness, he married a prostitute.

The Palm Sunday crowd, who were students of the Scriptures, knew these stories.

At first glance, this looked like a regular parade—the location, typical hoopla, procession, crowds—except for that upside-down curtain. Harvey Cox writes that in his entry into Jerusalem, Jesus "was lampooning imperial authority by bouncing into town, not on a prancing horse—the symbol of the warrior—but on a donkey, the peasant's plodding beast of burden."[54]

And dare one imagine that those who lined the streets may have been tipped off? Perhaps back in Galilee, days before this, neighbors whispered to neighbors, "Be on Main Street at such and such a time. You will want to be there." This was planned.

Right on Main Street, right amid the holy days leading up to the Passover, in symbolic action, Jesus offered a contrasting vision, another way. The way of the donkey.

Our creative challenge in our time, as in every time, is to find a donkey—a way to bring to the light and into question the dominant and controlling values of our time, and to picture an alternative way, a better way. Remember the Beatitudes—"Blessed are the meek. . . . Blessed are the poor in Spirit." In our time, in our society, in our settings, we are agents of another kingdom. We live in this world, but we are regularly introducing suggestions of a better way, a new kingdom.

I am delighted to report that all across this congregation there have been examples of persons choosing to ride a donkey. Let me tell briefly three stories.

More than a year ago, at Alderfer Auction Company, a man was hired whose employment record was less than stellar. But Sandy thought he deserved a chance. The man had an alcohol problem, and the company tried to work with him, making counseling available and more.

But the alcohol had control. The employee became a danger to himself and to others. Sandy needed to dismiss him.

Soon thereafter he committed suicide. No one took responsibility for any kind of memorial service—not the family, no church, no friends. So Sandy engaged Carl Yusavitz, pastoral counselor at Penn Foundation, to plan a service. It was held at Alderfer Auction Company with about sixty-five people present there to hear the words of comfort and hope. That is alternative vision.

Last week was Pastor's Day at Christopher Dock High School. Before the chapel service I stepped into a classroom. A video was being shown. It was the film "Romero"—the story of a Catholic priest who sided with the poor in El Salvador. He was labeled a Communist by the government and by the powerful elite of the country. Eventually he was killed. The Christopher Dock teacher stopped the film and asked the students, "What motivated this priest to risk his life to side with the poor? How does one explain this?" That is introducing an alternative vision.

A few years ago a family was in conflict. Among other issues there seemed to be some feelings that in property dealings the parents had not quite received a fair financial compensation. I was about to suggest that this matter be addressed by the family as we sat together. But before I could speak, the father with strength of voice and conviction said to his children, "Money means nothing to me. It is my family that matters." A donkey was on the street that day.

Many stories could be added. In countless ways in your daily lives you are finding ways to offer that creative approach, the unexpected twist, the "who-would-have-expected" action that offers ways to counter the dominant values of our time and suggests an alternative vision. Again and again, in wonderful, surprising, unexpected ways you introduce a donkey into the picture. And people pause to look.

Yes, we do participate in the parades. We are in the world. We buy and sell, work and play. We have not chosen to live in a monastery near some mountain. We have chosen to be in the mix of things. But right amid the routines of life, we do odd things. We have a curtain upside-down. We deliberately, with careful planning, introduce a donkey into the procession.

I hope and pray that the Christian church will find—amid the world's parades—new ways to stage a donkey ride. Amid the dominant values of consumerism, the notion that violence is a way to solve disputes, the triumph of "technique," I hope and pray for alternative visions to be offered. In a society where "success" is most often the operative goal, I hope we will have the courage and creativity to introduce into our lives and activities, into the parades on Market Street or Main Street, into our homes and churches, a donkey that captures the attention and points the way to the One who rode that donkey on Palm Sunday.

Chapter 29

You Will Be
My Witnesses

SERIES: SEEING GOD'S PRESENCE AND
SENSING GOD'S CALL IN THE RHYTHMS OF DAILY LIFE
May 29, 2005
Psalm 145:4-7; Luke 4:14-21; Acts 1:6-8

In an ordinary week, with how many persons do you speak? We might start with counting the check-out persons at Henning's Market, the neighbors next door, the colleagues at work. Would it be fifty? One hundred? Several hundred?

In recent weeks we have been addressing the theme of "Seeing God's Presence and Sensing God's Call in the Rhythms of Daily Life." Today I wish to have us consider our testimony, our witness in our daily interactions with others.

Witness, evangelism—the topic stirs up a variety of thoughts, does it not? We know we ought to do it, right? But we are afraid, do not know how, feel clumsy.

We have mixed feelings about those who give witness aggressively. The Jehovah's Witnesses are not our favorite visitors. We admire from a distance the dedication of the Mormons, but we are not sure we want to copy their methods.

A number of you remember the days of door-to-door tract distribution. Did you not generally go to places out of your own community, go down the streets and insert tracts in the doors, and move on—hopefully before anyone came to the door?

Many of us have not been fully comfortable with confrontational approaches such as "If you died tonight, would you go to heaven or hell?"

Knowing what not to do, and how not to witness, many or even perhaps most of us, conclude that witness and evangelism is not our gift. Some have that gift, but it is not ours.

Another way to sidestep this issue of witness is to suggest that we will let our lives speak. It is good, of course, for lives to do their own form of speaking. But some words added to the witness of our lives would be much better.

The Scriptures indeed suggest that we are all called to be witnesses. The great commission given to the disciples and, we believe, to us, is to—"Go . . . and make disciples of all nations. . . . " In John's Gospel, these were the words of Jesus to the disciples after his resurrection: "As the Father has sent me, so I send you." So to suggest that to witness is not our gift is to weasel out of our calling.

Perhaps we view witness too much as obligation. It is the good deed that we have to do. It's like as children taking cod liver oil—it tasted terrible, but it was good for you, so you did it.

Did you notice the text read from Acts 1? Does the text say, "You *must* be my witnesses. . . "? No, the text reports that the Holy Spirit will come upon you and "you *will* be my witnesses. . . . " Witness is not obligation—rather, it is explanation, it is testimony. Peter wrote in his letter to the early congregation: "Always be ready to make your defense to anyone who demands from you an accounting for the hope that is in you. . . " (1 Pet. 3:15b-16a).

Testimony is explanation of what makes us tick, why we live the way we do, how we explain our priorities, what it is that gives us joy, and so much more.

So then what do we say? To what do we give witness? Drawing from the text read, let me suggest several out of many possible ways to witness.

The writer of Psalm 145 put it in verse 6 like this: "The might of your awesome deeds shall be proclaimed, and I will declare your greatness." We give witness to the beauty and grandeur all around us. We live with what one writer calls an "abiding astonishment." Wonder, awe, adoration characterize our lives and our words. Worship is not simply a Sunday morning activity. Worship is a weeklong disposition.

Quite a few years ago the New Testament scholar J. B. Phillips wrote a book entitled *Your God Is too Small*. It seems to me that for many of our time the world is too small. There is a kind of thinness in people's lives. So we give testimony to the expansiveness of life, the beauty of our world, the amazing complexity of God's creation.

With better telescopes and microscopes, what do scientists see but more complexity, additional beauty, amazing symmetry and balance, and so much more? So we give witness regularly and consistently to beauty, to what is good, to the richness of life, to the experiences and possibilities of joy. Thankfulness, wonder, praise are the demeanor of our lives. To be sure, on certain days we might sing the songs of lost love, disappointment, and more, but most of the time our song is that "This Is My Father's World."

In our looking for beauty and goodness, let us not overlook each other. Amid some continuing differences of opinion here, some of us have been a little too hard on each other. We would do well to delight a bit more in each other's goodness.

Second, in our actions and words we give witness to the faith through our sharing Jesus' concerns. Our attention is consistently turned toward the vulnerable, the rejected, the neglected, those on the lower rungs of the economic ladder, the underprivileged. We treat with equal respect those whose names are honored and those quite nameless.

Thus, the checkout persons at the grocery store, the bank teller, the cleaning women—often persons of color still too often not accorded full dignity in our culture—in the hotels and motels are all seen as persons of dignity and worth and are treated as such. In our words of love, acceptance, and care we give testimony of God's love and compassion.

Painted on the rock ledges along highways from time to time we see words placed there by someone who obviously risked their safety to climb there to paint. The letters are often not even, the paint ran a bit. But the words are striking: "Jesus Saves." Sometimes in earlier years I wondered whether that was really the best way to give witness to the faith. Would people know what it meant? Would not more information be necessary? Perhaps so.

But we can fill out that brief message in our testimony, our witness. The message that we can offer gently or boldly, directly or indirectly, in lengthy conversation or over coffee, is that Jesus saves us from paths in life that simply go round and round. Jesus saves us from false gods. Jesus saves us from false promises. Jesus saves us from fear. Jesus calls us to visions bold and meaningful.

Now a word on the "how to" of our witness, the style of our testimony.

First, let us always recognize that we are not the ones called upon to convert others. We are to bear witness. It is the Spirit who calls.

So we do not give in to manipulation. We do not impose our views. We do not suggest that we are superior. Earlier I quoted from 1 Peter the Scripture that encourages us always to be ready to give an accounting for the hope that is in us. The text then adds the words, "yet do it with gentleness and reverence" (1 Pet. 3:16).

We are not called upon to argue down another. We are not directed to have the last word. We offer testimony.

In our witness we most often listen before we speak. We listen with Spirit-led ears and minds to hear what is behind the observations, questions, complaints, fears of others.

And we realize that not every occasion, not+ every conversation is the appropriate time for giving testimony. We are quite sensitive to the ebb and flow of people's lives. What is on their hearts and minds is what is of interest to us. It is not that on a given day we have a given number of persons to whom we must witness.

Jesus did not invite himself to lunch with every tax collector. But when he saw Zachaeus up in a tree, that provided the opportunity for inviting himself to the house of Zachaeus for lunch.

In our openness to the Spirit we sense when to speak.

In our witness and testimony we want to leave in people's minds that thought that lingers, the expression that has encouraged and honored them. Paul wrote in 2 Corinthians that "we are not peddlers of God's Word like so many, but in Christ we speak as persons of sincerity, as persons sent from God and standing in his presence." Earlier in the text Paul used the memorable imagery that "we are the aroma of Christ."

Have you ever listened to the program *Car Talk* on National Public Radio? You can call in your particular problem with your car, and these two humorous brothers seek to provide an answer.

Some years ago my brother Paul was on the program with his problem. It was actually a problem with my truck and my stock trailer. It was my problem, but my brother was on this national program.

I'll not go into the problem discussed. But the discussion went back and forth between my brother and these two gentlemen: "What do you haul in the trailer? How far do you travel?" On and on.

When the conversation had ended, and Paul was off the air, the one brother said to the other, "You know, that Paul seems like a nice guy. He seems like the kind of guy you would like to sit on the porch with and smoke a cigar."

At the conclusion of our witness, the next day, or the next week, that (maybe without the cigar!) is what we hope for: that a person will say, "You know, I would like to know more, to be with that person again. Something there looks inviting."

We are the aroma of Christ. Now that is a privilege.

Chapter 30

Like Those Who Dream

THIRD SUNDAY OF ADVENT
December 11, 2005
Psalm 126; Isaiah 61:1-4; John 1:6-8, 19-28

Some marriages—perhaps many—settle over a period of years into a predictable routine. Nothing is terribly wrong. The spouses are not in open conflict. There is no abuse. It is simply that day follows day, week follows week, in a kind of humdrum, low-energy existence.

You see couples like these in restaurants from time to time. The high point of conversation is reached, it seems, when they discuss what they plan to order. "What are you having? . . . I had that the last time. Maybe I'll try this. Are you having regular coffee or decaf?" After that comes staring out the window. The marriage is not terrible; it is just that there is little zing, expectation, drama.

The setting of the text read from Isaiah may have been Babylon. Many of the people of Israel had been there some seventy years. After the second or third generation, they had gotten rather settled. The memories of God's promises, of God's faithfulness in earlier centuries, were long gone—ancient history.

So Babylon was now home. They had settled in. Whatever Babylon offered appeared to be all there was. Their dreams, hopes, desires hardly rose above whatever the Babylonians extended them.

The wisdom of the day may well have been that this is it. Get used to it. Make a buck where you can. Live for the next vacation. What's on TV? Are you having regular or decaf?

So the prophet who would arouse these people out of their unimaginative conversation needed to speak with unusual power. Exceptional, imaginative, poetic language and musical cadence were needed. Thus, in the prophetic poetry again and again the words *awake, listen, hear, see* occur. "Sing, O barren one. . . . " "Ho, everyone who thirsts. . . . "

Many of the Advent texts are drawn from this exceptional poetry. "Comfort, comfort my people. Every valley shall be exalted, every hill made low, the crooked straight, the rough places a plain. His name shall be called Wonderful, Counselor, Mighty God, Prince of Peace."

So the words leap off the page. The heart begins to quicken. One begins to see children playing in the streets, gardens in bloom, water in dry streambeds.

What is so engaging about the Christmas story is the unexpected, the novel—so different, so wonderful. Who could have imagined? Would you believe!

But we must wonder—is this it? Wonderful as it is, is there no more? Shall we just keep celebrating this wonderful story? Has God exhausted the God-self in this Christ event?

When I studied at Baylor University years ago, I had a talented history professor, a graduate of an elite university. He had written one book. His colleagues and students always wondered why he had not written more. One book. That was it.

Did God have only one book to write? Was God finished after the incarnation? Shall our imagination be limited to finding new angles to tell this Bethlehem story, adding, as some seem to do, more glittery decorations each year?

The Christian faith suggests that there *is* much more. We believe in blessings yet to come, conversions yet to happen, hills still to be made low and valleys to be lifted up.

When God touches down, there are not minor adjustments in the human spirit, not simply feel-good results. Rather, there is good news, liberty, adjustment in the whole social reality.

Notice the change that the prophet envisioned when the servant of the Lord spoke the Word—

a garland instead of ashes,
oil of gladness instead of mourning,
mantle of praise instead of a faint spirit.

Ashes, mourning, faint spirit—regular or decaf. Do we too often wish for God on our terms, to fill our void, to meet our needs within our program, and miss the One who wills to do more? W. H. Auden in a poem has Herod the King speaking:

"O God, put away justice and truth for we cannot understand them and do not want them. . . . Leave the heavens
and come down . . . Become our uncle. Look after Baby,
amuse grandfather, escort Madam to the Opera, help Willy
with his homework, and introduce Muriel to a handsome
naval officer. Be interesting and weak like us, and we will
love you as we love ourselves."[55]

What is so remarkable, wonderful, about the Christmas story, indeed what is so remarkable and wonderful about the gospel message is that God does more and much better. The God we worship is the God of newness and difference.

In speaking of the Christian Peacemaker Team members being held in Iraq, Rush Limbaugh was reported to have said he was glad that these "leftist feel-good hand-wringers" were being "shown reality." There is enough reality around. We need something more.

In a poem "After Annunciation," Madeleine L'Engle wrote of an "irrational season" of "bright and wild love" and observed that "Had Mary been filled with reason / There'd have been no room for the child."[56]

When John the Baptist was holding forth across the Jordan, representatives of the religious establishment asked John whether he was speaking of someone who would fit into their religious categories, their system, their framework. Perhaps he was speaking of Elijah. Or perhaps another prophet.

John said, No way! The One of whom he spoke, he said, went beyond existing notions, perceptions, expectations. This One, John said, went way beyond. He would be unworthy to tie his shoe laces.

So again this Advent season we may wish to ponder whether our expectations, our hopes are imaginative enough.

Perhaps our prayers for God to meet our needs are too narrow. The wealth and health gospel is off the mark, far too limited. The notion that God meets us only on our terms is woefully, tragically small.

This is not the time for conventional wisdom. This is not the time for the old truisms like "You got to do what you got to do." This is not the time to suggest that we need to "get them before they get us." This is not the time to live in constant worry and anxiety.

Writing of our times, Charles Mendenhall wrote: "We lived in an 'age of anxiety' before 9-11. Now that anxiety has metasta-sized and flirts with paranoia in the deep recesses of our minds."[57] One might add that our government exploits this fear regularly.

We have inherited a counter-story. We sing a different tune.

This is the time to live in hope, expectation, faith. This is the time to stand in wonder, to host mystery. It is the time to ac-knowledge that God does not work in straight lines. With God all bets are off, all predictions inadequate. We can try to connect the dots, but God comes up with new configurations. This is the time to live by a new script.

This is the time for levels of conversation to transcend decaf or regular.

This is the time to remember and live our story: "When the Lord restored the fortunes of Zion, we were like those who dream."

When we remember and live our story, we pray "Thy king-dom come, Thy will be done on earth, as it is in heaven." And we believe this can happen.

Chapter 31

After You Leave

LABOR DAY WEEKEND
September 3, 2006
Matthew 6:19-21; 2 Corinthians 2:14-17

Earlier this year I attended a seminar at Princeton Theological Seminary on "Jihad, Holy War, and Just War." The seminar speakers were a Muslim scholar speaking on "Jihad," a Jewish scholar speaking on "Holy War," and a Christian scholar speaking on "Just War." Each speaker dealt with the question of under what conditions their tradition would find war permissible.

I was especially impressed by the presentation of the Jewish scholar. He was particularly helpful, in reviewing Israel's history, to note when war was permitted, when not permitted, who gave permission, and what the criteria for permission were. But what was even more impressive was his command of the English language. Rarely have I heard someone speak with such clarity, beauty, and rich vocabulary. Ellen had been with me at the seminar, and on the way home she commented, "I think that I just barely speak English."

Let me tell you of my friend Steve. I do not know his last name. He works at Dependable Motors in Honeybrook, Pennsylvania. Dependable Motors is a small farm machinery business.

Steve knows the workings of New Holland hay balers inside and out. Earlier this summer, on the first time around to bale a field of hay, my New Holland baler made a very bad sound and sheared a safety pin. I replaced the shear bolt; immediately it happened again. I had no idea what the trouble was, except that it appeared to be a big problem—"out of time," I told my brother.

I call my friend Steve. He knows me; I had called before. "It's a 316 baler, right?" he asks.

I say, "Right."

He asks, "Does it shear one bolt or also the one at the knotter?"

I respond, "It shears two." He says, "Good. It is not out of time."

He goes on that it could be a problem with the knotter. On occasion he says that the knotter slips, and that is a big problem. But he says this rarely happens on a 316. What is likely is that a stick or a stone is caught in the bale chamber, and when the nettles pass, it jams.

I say I will look. Lo and behold, I find a stick wedged in the bale chamber. I remove it. All is well. My sons tell me I owe Steve a tub of some Longacre's ice cream.

Tomorrow is Labor Day—a day to recognize the value of work. Today I wish to consider the coupling of work and Christians, or the demeanor or behavior of Christians at work. What are the qualities that might be expected of Christians in the workplace?

I have already spoken of one quality—*competence*, as exemplified by the Jewish scholar and also by my friend Steve. Whatever our job is, we will want to do it well. One of the seven deadly sins identified by Jewish and Christian thinkers is that of slothfulness. No one respects a person who performs inattentively; a person who is content with just getting by; someone who leaves the job half done. What we set our hearts and minds to do, we will want to do well.

Inherent in doing a job well is the disposition of *diligence*. Let me tell you of my friend Denny. The audio system here at Salford is overseen by Denny Wampole. That you know. What you perhaps do not know is the diligence with which Denny works at making certain that on a Sunday morning you can hear well.

With the changing and upgrading of the audio equipment in recent years, there have been some problems. This auditorium is wonderful acoustically for music but presents a challenge for the spoken word. There has been an echo as sound bounces off the walls and the curved ceiling at slightly different sequence. So

Denny has been here at church at 3:00 or 4:00 in the morning, working, testing, adjusting—trying to get the sound right. That is diligence

Another quality of the Christian on the job is that of *sensitivity*, which includes care and thoughtfulness. Let me tell you of my friend Eileen. She works in the recovery room at Grand View Hospital. When you come out from under anesthesia, and your mind is foggy, it is nice to see your spouse, parent, son, or daughter. But then you are most fortunate if the nurse who attends to you is Eileen. She is competent, reassuring, with just the right touch of humor. And if before you come to full awareness you say things that make no sense, she does not record, repeat, or publish what you said. That is Christian sensitivity.

On the job Christians understandably pay respect to those over them—the owner, manager, supervisor. But where the special quality of the Christian is seen is the relationship with those lower on the organizational chart. A measure of our Christian life may well be indicated by how we treat the secretary, the clean-up people, the cashiers, the waitresses—those overworked and the underpaid.

It would be a good exercise for all of us to work a few days incognito as the room cleaners at Best Western. Barbara Ehrenreich has written a book well worth reading, entitled *Nickel and Dimed: On (Not) Getting By in America*. It is her story of working for months at low-paying jobs. The Christian notices those who are often ignored.

The Christian's ears, eyes, and hearts are *turned to the vulnerable*. Let me tell you about my friend Joanna. She has been teaching in the North Penn School District—teaching children with serious learning challenges. But when Joanna speaks of these children, there is no tone of "difficult," no word of "handicapped." Rather she speaks of these children as special.

Now, of course, I could go up and down the church benches this morning, on the Delp House side and the Schoolhouse side, speaking of remarkable and wonderful qualities of the Christian faith exhibited every day, Monday to Friday, in your places of work. I could speak of volunteer work—Roy Musselman at Grand View, Jan Foderaro in volunteer chaplaincy work, Roma Ruth in hospice ministry, volunteers at the Care and Share shop, and so much more.

In the congregation here we rightly express appreciation for all who serve in the programs of the church. We would not have church were it not for the many persons offering their skills and experience in serving on boards and committees; teaching adults and children; serving as ushers, greeters, kitchen servers, song leaders, worship leaders, and more. We say thanks.

But the work of the kingdom is by no means confined to Sundays, nor confined to all the good work here. The work of the kingdom is Monday-Friday activity. In the workplace, on the soccer field, at the checkout counter at the grocery store—these are the places where the words, the thoughtfulness, the demeanor of the Christian has its effect and witness.

Sometimes I am asked, "What is Salford like?" I respond that anyone is invited to come here on a Sunday morning and experience the Salford congregation. But if you really want to know what Salford is like, you need to be with Salford people Monday through Friday.

We regularly pray, "Thy Kingdom come, thy will be done on earth as it is in heaven." The taste and smell of the kingdom is left by the quality of our words and actions, our comments and gestures.

On occasion, I'm sure, we have been recipients of angry words, sharpness of tongue, gestures indicating less than respect. In response, we have said to ourselves or perhaps to others, *I wonder where that came from?*

After we leave a situation, what might be the thoughts of those we have encountered? What aftertaste remains? Paul used this memorable image of leaving a fragrance—the "aroma of Christ," he called it.

What an opportunity and privilege is ours to everyday in encounter after encounter with others to leave a fragrance, to spread signs of the kingdom.

Chapter 32

To the Temple as Usual

FIRST SUNDAY AFTER CHRISTMAS, LAST SERMON AT SALFORD
December 31, 2006
I Samuel 2:18-20, 26; Luke 2:41-52

I doubt that the biblical writers went about their writing simply to tell a story, or that the details included in the narrative were meant only to add color or a little human interest. Rather, I believe what first appear as interesting little details were included in the narrative to teach, to inspire, to guide God's people.

In the texts read today, I wish for us to linger with three details that appear to be just little interesting touches but may well offer significant instruction. The first detail is that Hannah, mother of Samuel, would make and take each year to the temple a little robe. The second detail is in the Luke text, where the writer notes that the parents of Jesus went *as usual* to the festival. And the third little detail is the scene at the temple where Jesus both listens to the teachers and asks them questions. These three little pictures will serve as the foci for my musings this morning.

We have all been again blessed to experience and celebrate another Christmas. I suppose many of you have your special Christmas rituals and traditions. There is the special food family members can expect every Christmas. In about every family there is an aunt or uncle who every Christmas tells the same story again, and everyone laughs or cries as they did last year and the year before that. There are special Christmas decorations. It is these practices or rituals that create an identity, a sense of who you are as a family, a sense of belonging, a rooted-ness.

You noticed in the reading of the text from Luke that the family of Jesus went every year to Jerusalem for the festival. So of course when Jesus reached age twelve they "went up as usual to the festival."

There are practices, traditions, rituals that in our families and in the church should be usual, foundational, expected, routine—"that is the way we do things." Let me name three foundational practices for individuals and families, and you could very well add others.

Of course, it should be the usual practice for people to be in church. This is not primarily to please the preacher or make the singing stronger; it is rather a statement of who one is, a recognition of "Whose" one is, a statement of identity and allegiance.

Second, a usual practice should be that of stewardship. By the regular setting aside of money and time to be given, we routinely signify that we are the recipients of God's good gifts and blessings, and we remember that a calling from the beginning of time is to steward what we have been given.

Third, the discipline of Bible study, meditation, reflection, and prayer should be "as usual." With children we dare not neglect the reading of the Bible stories and conversations about the meaning of these stories.

As a congregation Salford has developed practices that are usual. These have wonderfully shaped the special quality and character of the congregation. I mention in particular the annual MDS team which "as usual" emphasizes the serving of others in need. I mention the regular volunteer work of many of you at the Thrift Shop. I mention the frequency with which young adults give a year or more of Voluntary Service.

The Seekers Class has undertaken to participate in the Agros Project in Guatemala. We have established a sister relationship with the Dios con Nosotros congregation in Mexico City. The first Tuesday evening and Wednesday of the month the Sewing Circle gathers. I could go on.

I turn now to the detail of Hannah annually making and taking a little robe to Samuel who, as you know, served in the temple. Here is a touching demonstration of a mother's love and attentiveness. The gesture also symbolizes at least two virtues.

First, it was Hannah and Elkanah's affirmation of Samuel's service to the faith. As parents, grandparents, sisters and brothers in the community of faith we need to affirm and encourage every step the young make to affiliate with and serve the church. Of course we affirm children in their artistic, academic, athletic, professional developments—but with special "robe-making" we want to affirm service to the Lord.

Second, Hannah's annual gesture required that each robe she made needed to be a little larger, for the text reads in verse 26 that "the boy Samuel continued to grow . . . in stature. . . . " Let there be at every level of our church life an expectation of growth in knowledge, growth in grace, growth in commitment and compassion. One of the great tragedies of the contemporary Christian church in America is that the church's "robe" has stayed about the same size. The church has moved in the direction of entertainment, meeting individual wishes and needs, a kind of light soup for the soul—a tendency toward the novel rather than the substantive. We may be ill-prepared for the future—of which I will say more in a moment. I fear the church's robe is too small.

The third image I call attention to in the text is that of Jesus in the temple, "sitting among the teachers, listening to them and asking them questions." In our regular pilgrimage to the temple, in our engagement with the biblical text, we need to consider what part of the Scripture we should engage in the time and context in which we live. So in the temple time we not only listen but must ask questions.

Our Scriptures are exceptionally rich in variety, emphases, angles of vision, and teachings. The writers of Scripture do not speak in a single voice; they do not all sing music in the same key; the concerns addressed are not all the same. Thus biblical scholars in recent years have emphasized the variety within Scripture. The words used to describe this are that the Bible is "thick," or "polyvalent," or "multi-dimensional."

Our task, our discerning task, is to consider which musical melodies, which biblical themes, which angles of vision need to be lifted up in our time if the Word of the Lord is to be fresh, compelling, and instructive for this setting in which we live. What are the biblical themes that need attention in our time?

Let me highlight several emphases that should receive attention now by suggesting two biblical books that in this era might receive careful consideration and two of the Ten Commandments that need renewed attention. You might be surprised at my selections.

The first biblical book that should receive renewed attention is Leviticus. On the face of it, this book looks entirely irrelevant for our time. And in one respect, it is. The specific suggestions are for all kinds of entirely outdated and odd (to us) restrictions, ritual acts of cleansing, food laws, clothing expectations, and much more. But it is the word and concept of *odd* that I'm after. Let me use a word that gives a far more positive cast to it—the word *distinctive*.

For the past fifty years, a little more than the span of the time in which I have been privileged to serve in the church, a deliberate trend among members of the Mennonite church, us included, has been to shed our oddity. To blend in has been a compelling desire. We have been tired of being embarrassed, of sticking out.

Now I have not been entirely unsympathetic to this movement. The specific choices of the church, the specific applications of the scriptural expectations, were not always wise in retrospect. Wearing black dresses, suits, and shoes did not necessarily have a biblical mandate, nor did it especially and compellingly communicate the message of Jesus.

I have no need to see the church return to a long list of legalisms and prohibitions, except to ask this question: Precisely where and in what ways *do* we suggest that the church stand aside from the culture in which we live? What practices, lifestyle decisions, and expectations might be set forth as clearly arising from the biblical vision and that will inevitably place us in tension with the dominant cultural values? Where will be our points of distinctiveness? Where and how will we be light and salt? If there is no difference, there is no message.

I find it quite interesting that a leader of what is termed the "emergent church," a church supposedly relevant to the times, commented recently about the Amish, saying, "I don't think anyone has ever done a better job of sharing the message of the gospel." Fascinating, is it not, that those who are the more odd are the more compelling in their witness.

So precisely how do we need to be odd or distinctive? Leviticus is not what we need to duplicate, but it helps us to focus the question.

That leads me to the second biblical book that deserves renewed attention. Surprise number two—the book of Revelation. No, I have not gotten caught up in the *Left Behind* novels; I do not see on the immediate horizon some battle of Armageddon. I'm not into some new video game put out by the Left Behind crowd in which those who are not Christians are knocked off.

I'm interested in the theme of the book of Revelation—how to live faithfully and hopefully when the tension between the church and the nation increases, when the nation begins to ask for allegiances which belong solely to God.

Like the church in the period of the writing of the book of Revelation, we live in the context of an empire—Roman in their case, American in ours. The church in the era of the writing of the book of Revelation viewed the Roman Empire in a negative, critical light—thus the imagery of Babylon, the beast, horns, and other odd images.

We live in a time and age when our empire is not viewed favorably by many peoples around the globe. The United States may well be an empire in the early stages of decline—a dangerous and vulnerable time. As a church we need to be able to see ourselves in greater tension with the nation than in decades past. Are we ready for that role of witness and prophetic critique?

Now, finally, two of the Ten Commandments needing special attention in our time—perhaps less of a surprise here.

The first one is not one of the "thou shalt not" commandments. Rather it is the "remember" commandment—"Remember the Sabbath Day." Israel had lived for decades in Egypt. There the dominant philosophy or ideology, the pervasive music in every media outlet, was "more bricks, more bricks"—seven days a week, "more bricks." Pharaoh had an insatiable need for bricks.

Israel had come out of Egypt and was on the way to the Promised Land. Now the counter-melody, the new music, was manna in the wilderness, enough for each day. And Jesus added a new hymn to that wonderful musical tradition in feeding the five thousand—a meal of which, when all had eaten their fill, there were twelve baskets left over. The contrast between Pharaoh and Jesus could not be more vividly drawn. With Pharaoh, never enough; with Jesus, plenty.

Sabbath is a time to remember that there is enough, and a time to worship and give thanks that we have been liberated from the crushing load of "more and more bricks" to the land of "more than adequate supply." So every Sabbath we gather to say thanks.

The second Commandment needing attention in our age is the last. Here is a "thou shalt not" theme. It is, "Thou shalt not covet." This also addresses the "more bricks" slavery.

Our society is well nigh consumed with getting more—more money, more power, more cars, more oil, more sports, more entertainment, more shopping. The outcome is now writ large in Iraq. Our nation has overreached and our leaders do not catch on. So the only option seen is more troops. It is Pharaoh all over again—"more bricks."

And in our world's insatiable reach for more and more, our planet is now on the verge of serious ecological consequences. The polar bears are endangered, and John and Susie Smith are more anxious and less satisfied. The commandments "Do not covet" and "Remember the Sabbath" offer liberation indeed.

Amid the topics of Leviticus, Revelation, Sabbath, and polar bears there is adequate agenda to occupy the discussions of twelve-year-olds and teachers and elders for the next few years.

But the conversation and discussion is best carried on intermingled with music and song. For the baptized community lives and thrives with a profound sense of joy and well-being, of faith and trust. To the world's longing for "more bricks," the baptized community has counter-music, doxology: "Oh, that I had a thousand voices to praise my God with thousand tongues." Let that music be the dominant sound in our lives and in the life of the community of faith.

Thus, we go to the temple as usual.

Appendix: Sermon Themes at Salford 1992-2006, Preached by James C. Longacre and Others

1992
May—Family Life Themes
September-November—Old Testament Personalities
December—Biblical Birth Stories

1993
February-March—Lent and Easter Texts
May-June—Spirituality for Life's Journey
August—Early Stories in Genesis
September-November—Wild and Wonderful Biblical Visions
December—Advent

1994
January—Issues of Christology
February-April—Lent and Easter Texts
May-June—Family Life Issues
September-November—Parables of the Kingdom
December—Advent

1995

January-February—Themes from the *Mennonite Confession of Faith*

March-April—Out of the Depths I Cry to Thee (Selections from the Psalms)

April-June—The Spiritual Family and the Biological Family

September-November—God's People in Ministry

December—Hope from Isaiah

1996

January-February—I and 2 Thessalonians

April-July—Being Anabaptist in the Twenty-first Century

September-October—Lord, Teach Us to Pray

December—Advent

1997

January—(Mennonite World Conference, Calcutta, India)

February—The Book of Esther

March—Revelation 2 and 3

April-May—The Jesus of History and the Christ of Faith: The Book of Colossians

June—Living Grace-filled Lives

September-November 1997—Compelling Biblical Images of the Church in Missions

December—Advent

1998

January-February—Selected Texts from Jeremiah and Ezekiel

March-April—Lent and Easter Texts

May-June—Astounding Biblical Visions, Promises, Expectations

September-November—Old Testament Personalities Seek to Understand God as Promise Maker and Covenant Partner

December—Advent—Great Invitations

1999

January-February—Parables

April-May—The Holy Spirit

June—Family Life Issues

September-November—Encouragement and Hope from the Images and Words of the Book of Revelation

December—Advent—How Far to Bethlehem?

2000

January-February—Counter Winds to the Faith

March-April—Lent and Easter Themes

May—Habits for Healthy Living

June-August—Doing What Comes Unnaturally

September-November—Hope in the Season of Despair (Isa. 40-55)

December—Advent/Christmas

2001

January-February—Compelling Biblical Invitations

March-April—Lent/Easter Themes

May-August—Living the Faith in Daily Life—A More Excellent Way

September-November—Galatians—One in Christ—The Message of Galatians

December—Advent/Christmas

2002

January-February—New Thoughts from Familiar Texts

March—Lent/Easter

May-August—The Style and Demeanor of the Christian

September-November—Imaginative Alternatives from Elijah and Elisha

December 2002—Advent/Christmas

2003

January-March—(Pastoral Sabbatical)

April—Lent/Easter

May-August—Holy Habits

September-November—From Jerusalem to Rome: Joys and Challenges Faced by the Early Church as found in the Book of Acts

December—Advent/Christmas

2004

January-February—Insiders and Outsiders: Ruth, Esther, Jonah

March—Lent/Easter

April-May—Tough Issues in the Christian Faith

June—The Christian Message and Society's Anxieties

September-November—Difficult Questions in the Faith

December—Advent/Christmas

2005

January-February—Sermon on the Mount

February-April—Lent

April-June—Seeing God's Presence and Sensing God's Call in the Rhythms of Daily Life

September-November—Deuteronomy

December—Advent/Christmas

2006

February—Building Dedication

March—Lent

June—Giving Witness to Our Faith

July—Relationships

September-November—Ephesians

December—Advent/Christmas

Notes

1. William Stacy Johnson, "Reading the Scripture Faithfully in a Postmodern Age," in *The Art of Reading Scripture*, ed. Ellen F. Davis and Richard B. Hays (Grand Rapids, Mich.: William B. Eerdmans Publishing Co., 2003), 115.

2. Richard Lischer, *The End of Words: The Language of Reconciliation in a Culture of Violence* (Grand Rapids, Mich.: William B. Eerdmans Publishing Company, 2005), 36.

3. Martin Luther King Jr., in Richard John Neuhaus, *Freedom for Ministry* (San Francisco: Harper & Row, 1979), 13.

4. Halford E. Luccock, "The Gospel According to St. Mark: Exposition," *The Interpreter's Bible*, vol. 7 (New York and Nashville: Abingdon Press, 1951), 865.

5. Henry Wadsworth Longfellow, *Kavanaugh, A Tale* (Boston: Ticknor, Reed and Fields, 1849), 10.

6. Helmut Thielicke, *I Believe: The Christian's Creed*, trans. John W. Doberstein and H. George Anderson (Philadelphia: Fortress Press, 1968), 127.

7. Tryon Edwards, quoted in Tryon Edwards, *The New Dictionary of Thoughts: A Cyclopedia of Quotations* (New York: Standard Book Company, 1954), 253.

8. A cluster of houses on the road between the Longacre farm at Bally and the Salford Meetinghouse at Harleysville.

9. James P. Martin, "Expository Article: Luke 1:39-47," *Interpretation* (October 1982): 397.

10. C. H. Dodd, in Walter Russell Bowie, *The Interpreter's Bible*, vol. 8 (New York and Nashville: Abingdon Press, 1952), 41.

11. Fred B. Craddock, *Luke*, in *Interpretation: A Bible Commentary for Teaching and Preaching*, ed. James L. Mays, Patrick D. Miller, and Paul J. Achtemeier (Louisville: John Knox Press, 1990), 30.

12. Mark Hillmer, "Between Text and Sermon: Luke 1:46-55," *Interpretation* (Oct. 1994): 392.

13. William Barclay, *The Daily Study Bible: The Gospel of Luke* (Edinburgh: The Saint Andrew Press, 1953), 10.

14. Anna Quindlen, "Public and Private; Every Day, Angels," *The New York Times*, Dec. 14, 1994.

15. *Confession of Faith in a Mennonite Perspective* (Scottdale, Pa.: Herald Press, 1995), 39.

16. William Barclay, *The Daily Study Bible: The Letters to the Galatians and Ephesians* (Edinburgh: The Saint Andrew Press, 1954), 125.

17. Barclay, 135.

18. Douglass John Hall, *Professing the Faith: Christian Theology in a North American Context* (Minneapolis: Fortress Press, 1993), 192.

19. John R. W. Stott, *The Message of Ephesians: God's New Society* (Leicester, England and Downers Grove, Ill.: Intervarsity Press, 1979), 110.

20. *Confession of Faith in a Mennonite Perspective*, 42.

21. Hall, *Professing*, 199.

22. Gordon D. Kauffman, *Systematic Theology: A Historicist Perspective* (New York: Charles Scribner's Sons, 1968), 482.

23. Hall, *Professing*, 192.

24. Stanley Hauerwas, *A Community of Character: Toward a Constructive Christian Social Ethic* (Notre Dame, Ind.: University of Notre Dame Press, 1981), 2.

25. Sara Wenger Shenk, "Remember Who You Are," *Mennonite Quarterly Review* (July 1995): 340.

26. Craddock, *Luke*, 90.

27. Pierre Teilhard de Chardin, *Writings*, selected with an introduction by Ursula King, Modern Spiritual Masters Series (Maryknoll, N.Y.: Orbis Books, 1999), 159.

28. Robert Coles, *The Story of Ruby Bridges* (Scholastic Press, 1995).

29. Walter Brueggeman, "Texts That Linger, Words That Explode," *Theology Today* (July 1997), 180.

30. Walter Brueggeman, *Texts under Negotiation: The Bible and Postmodern Imagination* (Minneapolis: Fortress Press, 1993), 88.

31. Mary Pipher, *The Shelter of Each Other* (New York: Ballantyne Books, 1996), 221.

32. Pipher, 225.

33. Thomas G. Long, "Learning to Speak of Sin," in *Preaching As a Theological Task: World, Gospel, Scripture: in Honor of David Buttrick*, ed. Thomas G. Long and Edward Farley (Louisville: Westminster John Knox Press, 1996), 102.

34. Willa Cather, *Death Comes for the Archbishop* (New York: Random House, 1936).

35. Lesslie Newbegin, *The Light Has Come: An Exposition of the Fourth Gospel* (Grand Rapids, Mich.: William B. Eerdmans Publishing Company, 1982), 120.

36. Edward Schillebeeckx, in Gerard Stephen Sloyan, *John: Interpretation: A Bible Commentary for Teaching and Preaching*, ed. James L. Mays, Patrick D. Miller, and Paul J. Achtemeier (Atlanta: John Knox Press, 1988), 115.

37. Reinhold Niebuhr, in James M. Wall, "Punishment for Sin," *Christian Century*, Oct. 28, 1998, 986.

38. Ellen T. Charry, "Spiritual Formation by the Doctrine of the Trinity," *Theology Today* (Oct. 1997): 370.

39. Charry, 370.

40. William Faulkner, *Absalom, Absalom!* (New York: Random House, 1936).

41. Palestinian Christians in Bethlehem, in e-mail message forwarded to author, week of Sept. 11, 2001.

42. Justice and Peace Committee of the Colombian Mennonite Church, in e-mail message forwarded to author, week of Sept. 11, 2001.

43. Evie and Wally Shellenberger, Mennonite Central Committee workers in Iran, in e-mail message forwarded to author, Sept. 13, 2001.

44. Martin Luther King, Jr., in Christine Pohl, "Profit and Loss," *Christian Century*, Aug. 29-Sept. 5, 2001, 13.

45. William H. Willimon, "World Makers: A New Way of Seeing and Naming," *The Christian Century*, Aug. 29-Sept. 5, 2001, 6.

46. Dom Helder Camara, *Through the Gospel with Dom Helder Camara* (New York: Orbis Books, 1986).

47. Thomas G. Long, "When Half Spent Was the Night: Preaching Hope in the New Millennium," *Journal for Preachers* 22 no. 3 (Easter 1999): 16-17.

48. Miroslav Volf, "Way of Life," *The Christian Century*, Nov. 20-Dec. 3, 2002, 35.

49. Walter Brueggemann, "Duty as Delight and Desire (Preaching Obedience That Is Not Legalism)," *Journal for Preachers* 18 no. 1 (Advent 1994): 3.

50. Barbara Brown Taylor, "Put on Faith," *The Christian Century*, July 17-30, 2002, 35.

51. Frederick Buechner, in John Timmer, "Owning Up to Baptism" in *A Chorus of Witnesses: Model Sermons for Today's Preacher*, ed. Thomas G. Long and Cornelius Plantinga, Jr. (Grand Rapids, Mich., William B. Eerdmans Publishing Company, 1994), 283.

52. Lewis B. Smedes, "What's God Up To? A Father Grieves the Loss of a Child," *The Christian Century*, May 3, 2003, 39.

53. Gordon Atkinson, "Following Red," *The Christian Century*, Dec. 14, 2004, 9.

54. Harvey Cox, *When Jesus Came to Harvard: Making Moral Choices Today* (Boston and New York: Houghton Mifflin Company, 2004), 213.

55. W. H. Auden, "For the Time Being: A Christmas Oratorio," quoted in Stephen R. Montgomery, "Beyond Fear, Fundamentalism, and Fox News: The Active Hope of Advent," *Journal for Preachers* 29 no. 1 (Advent 2005): 11.

56. Madeleine l'Engle, *The Irrational Season* (New York: The Seabury Press, 1977), 27.

57. Charles Mendenhall, "One New Book for the Preacher," *Journal for Preachers* 29 no. 1 (Advent 2005): 37.

The Author

James C. Longacre was born and raised on a family farm in Barto, Pennsylvania, the youngest of seven children. For the first five years of school, he attended a one-room school across the road from the farm. He is a graduate of Boyertown Area High School and Eastern Mennonite College (now University) in Harrisonburg, Virginia. He holds a Master of Arts degree from Baylor University in Waco, Texas.

An ordained Mennonite pastor, he has been a pastor in three Mennonite congregations. For six years he served as the Moderator of the Franconia Mennonite Conference and then for eleven years as the Franconia Mennonite Conference Coordinator.

Beyond the local Mennonite community he has also served on various churchwide Mennonite committees and boards, including the Mennonite Church General Board; the Theological Education Committee of the Mennonite Board of Education; the Mennonite Church Council on Faith, Life, and Strategy; and the Associated Mennonite Biblical Seminary Board of Directors. For six years he chaired the U. S. Peace Section of the Mennonite Central Committee.

Currently Longacre continues to farm and serves congregations as visiting preacher and teacher. He and his wife, Ellen Rose Herr Longacre, are the parents of three adult children.

Printed in the United States
128085LV00002B/14/P

9 781931 038515